Linux Administration

JASON CANNON

JASON CANNON

Contents

JASON CANNON

Other Books by the Author

Command Line Kung Fu: Bash Scripting Tricks, Linux Shell Programming Tips, and Bash One-liners
http://www.linuxtrainingacademy.com/command-line-kung-fu-book

High Availability for the LAMP Stack: Eliminate Single Points of Failure and Increase Uptime for Your Linux, Apache, MySQL, and PHP Based Web Applications
http://www.linuxtrainingacademy.com/ha-lamp-book

Linux for Beginners: An Introduction to the Linux Operating System and Command Line
http://www.linuxtrainingacademy.com/linux

Python Programming for Beginners: An Introduction to the Python Computer Language and Computer Programming
http://www.linuxtrainingacademy.com/python-programming-for-beginners

Introduction

After releasing my first book, *Linux for Beginners*, readers kept telling me, "I love Linux! It opened up a whole new world for me and I want to learn even more." Some even wanted to turn their newfound passion into a career as a Linux professional. "What's next?" they would ask.

I would point them to one of my courses or suggest they take a Linux system administration class. "That's great, but what *book* should I read next? What *book* would be a great companion to a Linux administration course?" I didn't have a good answer for them.

Most of the books on Linux system administration, as great as they are, are simply outdated. They all seem to come from a time when Linux more closely resembled Unix. Even recently released books didn't cover the fundamental shift in how system services are started and managed on modern Linux systems. With every year that passes, every new version of the Linux kernel that is released, and every new Linux distribution update, Linux looks less and less like a traditional Unix system. Now, more than ever before, Linux has to be treated as its own entity.

Now when someone asks me, "What book should I read next?", I have an answer for them. It's this book. This book is the next step after you understand how to use a Linux system. It teaches you how to *manage* a Linux system like a Linux system.

If you're ready to take that next step, let's get started.

Jason

Booting

As a system administrator you need to understand the Linux boot process. In this chapter, you will learn about the BIOS, the boot loader, the Linux kernel and runlevels.

The BIOS

BIOS stands for Basic Input/Output System. It's a special type of firmware used in the booting process and it's the first piece of software that is run when a computer is powered on. The BIOS is operating system independent. Its primary purpose is to test the underlying hardware components and to load a boot loader or operating system.

The BIOS performs a POST, which stands for Power-On Self Test. The POST performs some basic checks of various hardware components such as the CPU, memory, and storage devices. Only if the POST succeeds will the BIOS attempt to load the boot loader.

The BIOS contains a list of boot devices such as hard disks, a DVD drive, USB devices, and others depending on the hardware being used. The BIOS searches that list for a bootable device in the order specified. You can change this order by interrupting the boot sequence and entering into the configuration for the BIOS. The key combination used to do this will vary from one hardware manufacturer to another.

Once a bootable device has been found, the BIOS will run the boot loader. Typically the GRUB boot loader will be used, but you may run into older Linux systems that use the LILO boot loader. LILO stands for **LI**nux **LO**ader, while GRUB stands for **GR**and **U**nified **B**ootloader. In any case, the primary purpose of the boot loader is to start the operating system. You will typically see a message or series of messages from the boot loader which will allow you to interrupt the boot process and interact with the boot loader. If there are multiple operating systems installed, you can tell the boot loader which operating system to run. You can also instruct the boot loader to pass different boot options to the operating system.

The Initial RAM Disk

The initial RAM disk, abbreviated as "initrd," is a temporary file system that's loaded into memory when the system boots. This file system can contain helpers that perform hardware detection and load the necessary modules, sometimes called drivers, to get the actual file system mounted. For example, if the root file filesystem is stored on an LVM (Logical Volume Manager) volume, the initrd image will contain the kernel modules required to mount that logical volume as the root file system. Once the initrd mounts the actual root file system its job is done and the operating system continues loading from the real root file system.

Kernel and Initial RAM Disk Location

The Linux kernel, the initial RAM disk, and other files needed to boot the operating system are stored in **/boot**. Here is a listing of the **/boot** directory for an Ubuntu system.

```
$ ls -1F /boot
abi-3.13.0-46-generic
config-3.13.0-46-generic
grub/
initrd.img-3.13.0-46-generic
System.map-3.13.0-46-generic
vmlinuz-3.13.0-46-generic
```

The Linux kernel is typically named **vmlinux** or **vmlinuz**. If the kernel is compressed its name is in the **vmlinuz** format. In this example, the kernel is **vmlinuz-3.13.0-46-generic**. The initial RAM disk in this example is **initrd.img-3.13.0-46-generic**.

The Kernel Ring Buffer

The kernel ring buffer contains messages related to the Linux kernel. A ring buffer is a data structure that is always the same size. Once the buffer is completely full, old messages are discarded when new messages arrive. To see the contents of the kernel ring buffer, use the **dmesg** command.

```
$ dmesg
[    0.000000] Initializing cgroup subsys cpuset
[    0.000000] Initializing cgroup subsys cpu
[    0.000000] Initializing cgroup subsys cpuacct
[    0.000000] Linux version 3.13.0-46-generic
(buildd@orlo) (gcc version 4.8.2 (Ubuntu 4.8.2-
19ubuntu1) ) #79-Ubuntu SMP Tue Mar 10 20:06:50 UTC
2015 (Ubuntu 3.13.0-46.79-generic 3.13.11-ckt15)
[    0.000000] Command line:
BOOT_IMAGE=/boot/vmlinuz-3.13.0-46-generic
root=UUID=736134da-c6b8-4a97-911c-650146a68b3c ro
console=tty1 console=ttyS0
[    0.000000] KERNEL supported cpus:
[    0.000000]    Intel GenuineIntel
[    0.000000]    AMD AuthenticAMD
[    0.000000]    Centaur CentaurHauls
[    0.000000] e820: BIOS-provided physical RAM map:
...
```

On most Linux distributions these messages are also stored on disk in the **/var/log/dmesg** file. Between the **dmesg** command and the **/var/log/dmesg** log file, you will be able to see the messages the kernel is generating, even during the earliest stages of the boot process when those messages can quickly fly by your screen.

Runlevels and Targets

Linux uses runlevels to determine what processes and services to start. Each distribution can be configured differently, but, in general, runlevel 0 is used to power off a system, runlevel 1 is single-user mode, runlevels 2-5 are for normal system operations, and runlevel 6 is used to reboot a system.

```
Runlevel   Description
0          Shuts down the system
1, S, s    Single user mode. Used for maintenance.
2          Multi-user mode with graphical interface.
           (Debian/Ubuntu)
3          Multi-user text mode (RedHat/CentOS)
4          Undefined
5          Multi-user mode with graphical interface.
           (RedHat/CentOS)
6          Reboot
```

Historically, runlevels were controlled by the **init** program. The **init** configuration was stored in **/etc/inittab**. To change the default runlevel using **init**, you would edit the **/etc/inittab** file and set the runlevel number on the **initdefault** line. Here is an example of setting runlevel 3 to be the default runlevel.

```
id:3:initdefault:
```

However, **init** alternatives such as **systemd** and **upstart** are quickly taking the place of **init** with **systemd** currently being the most widely adopted replacement.

Instead of runlevels, **systemd** has the concepts of targets. These targets are roughly equivalent to runlevels. To see a list of available targets, look in **/lib/systemd/system**. You'll notice the runlevel targets are actually symlinks to the real targets being used. For example, **runlevel5.target** is a symlink to **graphical.target**.

```
# cd /lib/systemd/system
# ls -l runlevel*target
lrwxrwxrwx. 1 root root 15 Jul 17  2014
runlevel0.target -> poweroff.target
lrwxrwxrwx. 1 root root 13 Jul 17  2014
runlevel1.target -> rescue.target
lrwxrwxrwx. 1 root root 17 Jul 17  2014
runlevel2.target -> multi-user.target
lrwxrwxrwx. 1 root root 17 Jul 17  2014
runlevel3.target -> multi-user.target
lrwxrwxrwx. 1 root root 17 Jul 17  2014
runlevel4.target -> multi-user.target
lrwxrwxrwx. 1 root root 16 Jul 17  2014
runlevel5.target -> graphical.target
lrwxrwxrwx. 1 root root 13 Jul 17  2014
runlevel6.target -> reboot.target
```

To change the default runlevel, or target, with **systemd**, use the **systemctl** command followed by **set-default** and finally the desired target. Optionally, you can manually create a symlink to the desired target from the **/etc/systemd/system/default.target** file. This example sets the default target to be graphical, which is equivalent to runlevel 5.

```
# set-default multi-user.target
rm '/etc/systemd/system/default.target'
ln -s '/usr/lib/systemd/system/multi-user.target'
'/etc/systemd/system/default.target'
#
```

Changing Runlevels or Targets

With the init system, you can change runlevels using the **telinit** command. Simply supply the runlevel you want to change to as an argument to the **telinit** command.

```
# telinit 5
```

To change the target, the runlevel equivalent for **systemd**, use the **systemctl** command followed by **isolate** and finally the desired target. Here is how to change to the graphical target.

```
systemctl isolate graphical.target
```

Rebooting a System

Even though there is a runlevel/target if you're using **systemd**, for rebooting you can also use the **reboot** or **shutdown** commands.

Here's how to reboot with **init**.

```
# telinit 6
```

To reboot using **systemd** use the **systemctl** command.

```
# systemctl isolate reboot.target
```

To reboot using the **reboot** command simply execute **reboot.**

```
# reboot
```

The format of the **shutdown** command is as follows.

```
shutdown [options] time [message]
```

The option to tell **shutdown** to perform a reboot is **-r**. You can specify the time to shutdown using the "HH:MM" format. You can also use **+N** where **N** represents the number of minutes to wait before performing the action. Finally, you can use the **now** keyword to start immediately. Optionally, you may specify a message that will be broadcast to all users logged into the system.

```
# shutdown -r now
```

Powering Off a System

To power off a system, use runlevel 0, the poweroff target, or the poweroff command.

Here is how to issue a power-off with init.

```
# telinit 0
```

Here is how to power off a system with **systemctl**.

```
# systemctl isolate poweroff.target
```

Finally, you can use the **poweroff** command.

```
# poweroff
```

Summary

In this chapter, you learned about the Linux boot process. You learned that the job of the BIOS is to perform basic hardware checks and to start the boot loader from a bootable device. You also learned about the two most commonly used bootloaders, LILO and Grub. The primary job of any boot loader is to start the operating system.

You also learned that the files required to boot a Linux system are stored in the /boot directory. The initial ram disk, or initrd, is a tempory file system that is loaded into memory. Its main job is to mount the file system where the operating system is stored. The Linux kernel is typically named vmlinux, or, if it is compressed, vmlinuz.

You learned how to view the messages in the kernel ring buffer by using the dmesg command or by examining the /var/log/dmesg file.

You also learned about run levels and how systemd has an equivalent concept known as targets. You learned how to change the runlevel with the **telinit** command for the traditional init system, and the **systemctl** command for systems the use system. Finally, you learned about the shutdown, reboot, and poweroff commands.

Quiz

1. The BIOS begins the computer's boot process and passes control to the boot loader.

    a. True

    b. False

2. Which of the following are Linux boot loaders?

    a. LILO

    b. GRUB

    c. Both LILO and GRUB

    d. BIOS

3. Which of the following is a temporary file system which is loaded into memory when the system boots.

    a. kernel

    b. vmlinux

    c. vmlinuz

    d. initrd

4. The /linux directory contains the files required to boot Linux.

    a. True

    b. False

5. Which command displays the contents of the kernel ring buffer?

a. ringbuf

b. ringb

c. rmesg

d. dmesg

Quiz Answers

1. A

2. C

3. D

4. B

5. D

System Logging

Linux uses the syslog standard for message logging. This allows programs and applications to generate messages that can be captured, processed, and stored by the system logger. It eliminates the need for each and every application having to implement a logging mechanism. It also means that logging can be configured and controlled in a central location.

The syslog standard uses facilities and severities to categorize messages. Each message is labeled with a facility code and a severity level. The various combinations of facilities and severities can be used to determine how a message is handled.

Facilities are used to indicate what type of program or what part of the system the message originated from. For example, messages that are labeled with the **kern** facility originate from the Linux kernel. Messages that are labeled with the **mail** facility come from applications involved in handling mail.

Each facility has a number and a keyword associated with it. This table lists the syslog facilities.

Number	Keyword	Description
0	kern	kernel messages
1	user	user-level messages
2	mail	mail system
3	daemon	system daemons
4	auth	security/authorization messages
5	syslog	messages generated by syslogd
6	lpr	line printer subsystem
7	news	network news subsystem
8	uucp	UUCP subsystem
9	clock	daemon
10	authpriv	security/authorization messages
11	ftp	FTP daemon
12	-	NTP subsystem
13	-	log audit
14	-	log alert
15	cron	clock daemon
16	local0	local use 0 (local0)
17	local1	local use 1 (local1)
18	local2	local use 2 (local2)
19	local3	local use 3 (local3)
20	local4	local use 4 (local4)
21	local5	local use 5 (local5)
22	local6	local use 6 (local6)
23	local7	local use 7 (local7)

This table lists each of the severities, including their code, keyword, and description.

Code	Severity	Keyword	Description
0	Emergency	emerg (panic)	System is unusable
1	Alert	alert	Action must be taken immediately
2	Critical	crit	Critical conditions
3	Error	err (error)	Error conditions
4	Warning	warning (warn)	Warning conditions
5	Notice	notice	Normal but significant condition
6	Info	info	Informational messages
7	Debug	debug	Debug-level messages

A syslog server accepts syslog messages and process those messages based on a set of configurable rules. Traditionally, the **syslogd** daemon filled this role, but many Linux distributions today ship with alternatives such as **rsyslog** and **syslog-ng**. For the remainder of this chapter, we are going to focus on **rsyslog**; however, the concepts apply to any syslog server.

Logging Rules

The main configuration file for rsyslog is **/etc/rsyslog.conf**. You can include additional configuration files by using the **$IncludeConfig** directive. For example, this line will cause rsyslog to read and include all the configuration files that end in **.conf** in the /etc/rsyslog.d directory.

```
$IncludeConfig /etc/rsyslog.d/*.conf
```

Logging rules consist of two fields. The first field is called the selector field and it lists the facilities and severities of messages to include in the rule. The second field is called the action field and it determines what will happen to the messages matched by the selector field. The most common action is to write the messages to a log file. The selector field and action field can be separated by one or more spaces or tabs.

The format of the selector field is **FACILITY.SEVERITY**. Note that wildcards are supported. For example, use the **mail.*** selector to match all the mail messages. You can also omit the **.SEVERITY** if you want to include all messages from the facility. In short, **mail.*** and **mail** are equivalent. If you do not want to match any messages from a facility use **FACILITY.none**. If you want to match multiple facility/severity pairs, separate each pair with a semicolon.

This example rule matches messages that have the facility of **mail** and any severity. It writes all the matching messages to **/var/log/mail.log**.

```
mail.*      /var/log/mail.log
```

If the path starts with a minus sign that tells rsyslog that it doesn't have to perform a **sync()** operation for each log message. This is sometimes called caching mode. When using caching mode, know that some message might be lost if a system crashes immediately after a write attempt. However, you may see performance improvements during normal operations if you have a system that performs many logging operations. The default configurations that ship with a Linux distribution will probably have a mix of caching (-/path) and non-caching (/path) rules with less critical messages using caching. Here's an example.

```
mail.*      -/var/log/mail.log
```

In this example, there are separate actions for different severities of mail messages. Notice that the less critical mail messages are using caching mode.

```
mail.info      -/var/log/mail.info
mail.warn      -/var/log/mail.warn
mail.err       /var/log/mail.err
```

This example is taken from an Ubuntu system. The first line ensures all messages from the **auth** and **authpriv** facilities are written to **/var/log/auth.log**. The second line writes all messages except ones originating from the **auth** and **authpriv** facilities to /var/log/syslog.

```
auth,authpriv.*                /var/log/auth.log
*.*;auth.none,authpriv.none    -/var/log/syslog
```

This example is taken from a RedHat Enterprise Linux system. The rule tells rsyslog to write all messages except **mail**, **authpriv**, and **cron** to **/var/log/messages**.

```
*.info;mail.none;authpriv.none;cron.none /var/log/messages
```

Hopefully you can see why it's important to understand how to determine where messages are being sent instead of simply memorizing that system messages are stored in /var/log/messages. Different distributions ship with different configurations and different companies, organizations, and system administrators may alter the default rules to suit their particular needs.

Creating Your Own Syslog Messages

You can use the **logger** command to generate syslog messages. This can prove useful if you want to test any configuration changes you've made to the system logger or if you want to generate log message from your own shell scripts. Use the **-p** option to provide a **FACILITY.SEVERITY** level. If you don't specify a facility/severity pair, it will default to **user.notice**. You can also use the **-t** option to tag your message.

```
logger [options] message
```

In this example, we generate a message with the mail facility at a severity level of **info**. You can see that the message made its way to the proper log file.

```
$ logger -p mail.info -t mailtest "Testing 123."
$ sudo tail -1 /var/log/mail.log
Apr  4 14:33:16 linuxsvr mailtest: Testing 123.
```

Rotating Log Files

You can use the **logrotate** tool to rotate, compress, remove, and even mail log files. This provides an automated way to manage log files and can help prevent filling up your storage space with log messages.

The configuration file for **logrotate** is located at **/etc/logrotate.conf**. Like many other configuration files it may use an **include** directive. This line tells **logrotate** to read configuration files located in the **/etc/logrotate.d** directory.

```
include /etc/logrotate.d
```

Here is a sample **logrotate.conf** file.

```
# see "man logrotate" for details
# rotate log files weekly
weekly
```

```
# keep 4 weeks worth of backlogs
rotate 4

# create new (empty) log files after rotating
# old ones
create

# uncomment if you want your log files compressed
#compress

# packages drop log rotation information
# into this directory
include /etc/logrotate.d
```

The configuration in the main file contains some defaults. For example, the **weekly** keyword ensures that log files will be rotated every week. The **rotate 4** line tells logrotate to keep 4 weeks worth of logs. Logs older than this will be removed. The **create** line makes sure that a new empty log file is created after it is rotated.

This is a sample logrotate configuration file from an Ubuntu system. It is located at **/etc/logrotate.d/rsyslog**. It handles the log rotation for all the files associated with **rsyslog**.

```
/var/log/syslog
{
        rotate 7
        daily
        missingok
        notifempty
        delaycompress
        compress
        postrotate
                reload rsyslog >/dev/null 2>&1 || true
        endscript
}

/var/log/mail.info
/var/log/mail.warn
```

```
/var/log/mail.err
/var/log/mail.log
/var/log/daemon.log
/var/log/kern.log
/var/log/auth.log
/var/log/user.log
/var/log/lpr.log
/var/log/cron.log
/var/log/debug
/var/log/messages
{
        rotate 4
        weekly
        missingok
        notifempty
        compress
        delaycompress
        sharedscripts
        postrotate
                reload rsyslog >/dev/null 2>&1 || true
        endscript
}
```

Notice that the format is a single log file, or list of log files, followed by the configuration that controls those log files.   The configuration is enclosed in brackets. Here are the configuration options used.

rotate count   Rotate the files by **count** times before removing them.

daily   Rotate log files every day.

weekly   Rotate log files weekly.

missingok   Ignore missing log files. (Do not issue an error.)

notifempty   Do not rotate the log file if it is empty.

compress   Compress rotated log files.

postrotate   The lines between **postrotate** and **endscript** are executed using **/bin/sh**. These commands are executed after the rotation.

Testing Your Logrotate Configuration

If you make changes to your **logrotate** configuration and want to test it, use the following command.

```
# logrotate -fv /etc/logrotate.conf
```

The **-f** option tells **logrotate** to force a rotation while the **-v** option enables verbose logging.

Summary

In this chapter, you learned about the syslog standard and how it assigns a facility and severity to each message. You also learned that syslog servers employ the use of logging rules to determine what action to perform on a given message. Typically, the action is to simply store the message in a log file. You also learned how to test the syslog server configuration by generating messages with the **logger** utility. Finally, you learned how to use **logrotate** to automatically prune system logs.

Quiz

1. The syslog standard:

    a. Aids in the processing of messages.

    b. Allows logging to be centrally controlled.

    c. Uses facilities and severities to categorize messages.

    d. All of the above.

2. Which command can you use to generate log messages?

    a. logger

    b. log

    c. logit

    d. There is no such command.

Quiz Answers

1. D

2. A

Disk Management

When a disk or storage device is "partitioned" it is divided into parts. Each one of these parts is called a partition. Partitioning a disk allows you to allocate different sections of the disk for different purposes.

As a system administrator, you can decide what partitioning scheme to use. For example, you could use four partitions, allocating one partition for the operating system data, another partition for the application data, yet another one for the user data, and finally a partition dedicated to swap space. Another example scheme would simply be to use two partitions and separate the user's home directories from the rest of the system.

Having separate partitions is one way to prevent one part of the system from adversely affecting another part of the system. Having a dedicated partition for user home directories, for example, prevents a user from filling up the entire disk and interfering with the normal operation of the operating system. Even though a user, or group of users, may fill up the storage allocated for home directories and prevent another user from using more space, the operating system and any applications that are running will still be able to function normally. If this system hosts a website, the operating system will continue to run as well as the web server and a service outage will have been avoided.

The MBR Partitioning Scheme

The MBR, or master boot record, is a boot sector at the beginning of a storage device. The partition table that resides in the MBR contains information on how the logical partitions are organized on the disk. Because the partition table in the MBR can only address storage space up to 2 TB, it is being replaced by the GUID Partition Table (GPT).

The MBR partitioning scheme allows for up to four primary partitions. If you want to create more than four partitions, you'll need to use an extended partition. An extended partition is a special kind of primary partition that is used as a container for other partitions. This allows you to create an unlimited number of logical partitions.

The GUID Partition Table (GPT)

The GUID (global unique identifier) Partition Table, or GPT for short, is replacing the older MBR partitioning system. It is part of the Unified Extensible Firmware Interface (UEFI) standard. The UEFI is replacing the traditional BIOS; however, GPT has been used on some BIOS systems primarily due to the disk size limitations of MBR partition tables.

There are no primary and extended partitions with GPT. Using the default configuration, GPT supports up to 128 partitions. Also, GPT supports storage devices up to 9.4 ZB. The primary downside of GPT is is that it is not supported on older operating systems. Also, you'll need to use newer partitioning utilities that support GPT.

Mount Points

A mount point is simply a directory that is used to access the data on a partition. At minimum, there will be one partition mounted on the **/** mount point. Any additional partitions will be mounted on mount points below **/** in the directory tree. For example, if you allocated a partition for user home directories, that partition would be mounted at **/home**. The files and directories that are at or below the **/home** mount point will reside on that partition. For example, the files in my home directory, **/home/jason**, will be on the partition mounted at **/home**.

If you were to disconnect, or unmount, that partition and mount it to another directory (mount point), all the data would be available at that new mount point. If **/home** were unmounted and the partition was then mounted at **/export/home**, the files in my home directory would become available at **/export/home/jason**.

It's important to point out that you can mount partitions over existing data. For example, if files are created in **/home** before **/home** is mounted, those files will not be accessible. Let's say you only have the **/** partition mounted and you create a home directory for Sarah at **/home/sarah**. The directory **/home/sarah** resides on the partition that is mounted on **/**. If you were to then mount another partition on **/home**, you would no longer be able to access the **/home/sarah** directory. The data for **/home/sarah** still exists, but it is on the partition associated with **/**. Once you unmounted **/home** you would then see that **/home/sarah** still exists.

You can mount partitions anywhere in the Linux directory tree. You can even have mount points that reside on other mounted partitions. Let's say you have a partition mounted on **/home**. You could then mount yet another partition on **/home/jason**. It's important that **/home** be mounted before **/home/jason**. You'll learn how to associate partitions with mount points as well as control the order that partitions are mounted later in this chapter.

Creating Partitions

When performing interactive Linux installations you will most likely end up using a partitioning tool provided by the Linux distribution. However, if you want to manipulate disks after the initial installation you will most likely need to use a standard Linux tool. The **fdisk** utility has been traditionally used to create and modify partitions on a disk, but there are other viable alternatives including **gdisk** and **parted**. Earlier version of **fdisk** lacked support for GPT, but, as of this writing, **fdisk** supports GPT. To manage the partitions on a disk with **fdisk**, simply provide the path to the device you wish to manage as an argument to the command.

```
# fdisk /dev/sdb
Welcome to fdisk (util-linux 2.23.2).

Changes will remain in memory only, until you decide to
write them.
Be careful before using the write command.

Device does not contain a recognized partition table
Building a new DOS disklabel with disk identifier
0x1c0ae930.

Command (m for help): q

#
```

If you are unsure what disks are available, run **fdisk -l** to display a list of devices. This server has two disks. The first disk, **/dev/sda**, has already been partitioned and the second disk, **/dev/sdb**, has not.

```
# fdisk -l

Disk /dev/sda: 214.7 GB, 214748364800 bytes, 419430400
sectors
Units = sectors of 1 * 512 = 512 bytes
Sector size (logical/physical): 512 bytes / 512 bytes
I/O size (minimum/optimal): 512 bytes / 512 bytes
Disk label type: dos
Disk identifier: 0x000ad6ec
```

```
    Device Boot       Start          End       Blocks      Id
System
/dev/sda1              2048      4098047      2048000      82
Linux swap / Solaris
/dev/sda2     *      4098048    417794047    206848000     83
Linux

Disk /dev/sdb: 549.8 GB, 549755813888 bytes, 1073741824
sectors
Units = sectors of 1 * 512 = 512 bytes
Sector size (logical/physical): 512 bytes / 512 bytes
I/O size (minimum/optimal): 512 bytes / 512 bytes


#
```

Let's choose to work with **/dev/sdb** and ask **fdisk** for some help by typing in **m**.

```
# fdisk /dev/sdb
Welcome to fdisk (util-linux 2.23.2).

Changes will remain in memory only, until you decide to
write them.
Be careful before using the write command.

Device does not contain a recognized partition table
Building a new DOS disklabel with disk identifier
0xde069e1a.

Command (m for help): m
Command action
   a   toggle a bootable flag
   b   edit bsd disklabel
   c   toggle the dos compatibility flag
   d   delete a partition
   g   create a new empty GPT partition table
   G   create an IRIX (SGI) partition table
   l   list known partition types
   m   print this menu
   n   add a new partition
   o   create a new empty DOS partition table
   p   print the partition table
   q   quit without saving changes
   s   create a new empty Sun disklabel
   t   change a partition's system id
```

```
    u   change display/entry units
    v   verify the partition table
    w   write table to disk and exit
    x   extra functionality (experts only)

Command (m for help):
```

The following example demonstrates how to create a new MBR partition table. We will create three primary partitions. The first one will be a 1GB swap partition, the second will be a 20GB partition, and the final partition will use the remaining space on the disk.

To create a new MBR partition, type **n**. You will then be guided through a series of prompts which are fairly self-explanatory. The default partition type created by **fdisk** is Linux represented by 0x83. To change the partition type, type in **c**. The swap partition is represented by 0x82. To get a list of partition types, type l. To view the current partition table, use **p** and to write your changes to disk use **w**.

```
# fdisk /dev/sdb
Welcome to fdisk (util-linux 2.23.2).

Changes will remain in memory only, until you decide to
write them.
Be careful before using the write command.

Device does not contain a recognized partition table
Building a new DOS disklabel with disk identifier
0x6a290d93.

Command (m for help): n
Partition type:
    p   primary (0 primary, 0 extended, 4 free)
    e   extended
Select (default p): p
Partition number (1-4, default 1):
First sector (2048-1073741823, default 2048):
Using default value 2048
Last sector, +sectors or +size{K,M,G} (2048-1073741823,
default 1073741823): +1G
Partition 1 of type Linux and of size 1 GiB is set

Command (m for help): t
```

```
Selected partition 1
Hex code (type L to list all codes): 82
Changed type of partition 'Linux' to 'Linux swap / Solaris'

Command (m for help): n
Partition type:
   p   primary (1 primary, 0 extended, 3 free)
   e   extended
Select (default p):
Using default response p
Partition number (2-4, default 2):
First sector (2099200-1073741823, default 2099200):
Using default value 2099200
Last sector, +sectors or +size{K,M,G} (2099200-1073741823,
default 1073741823): +20G
Partition 2 of type Linux and of size 20 GiB is set

Command (m for help): n
Partition type:
   p   primary (2 primary, 0 extended, 2 free)
   e   extended
Select (default p):
Using default response p
Partition number (3,4, default 3):
First sector (44042240-1073741823, default 44042240):
Using default value 44042240
Last sector, +sectors or +size{K,M,G} (44042240-1073741823,
default 1073741823):
Using default value 1073741823
Partition 3 of type Linux and of size 491 GiB is set

Command (m for help): p

Disk /dev/sdb: 549.8 GB, 549755813888 bytes, 1073741824
sectors
Units = sectors of 1 * 512 = 512 bytes
Sector size (logical/physical): 512 bytes / 512 bytes
I/O size (minimum/optimal): 512 bytes / 512 bytes
Disk label type: dos
Disk identifier: 0xf22b19b6

    Device Boot       Start         End       Blocks    Id
System
/dev/sdb1            2048     2099199     1048576    82
Linux swap / Solaris
/dev/sdb2         2099200    44042239    20971520    83
```

```
Linux
/dev/sdb3        44042240  1073741823   514849792   83
Linux

Command (m for help): w
The partition table has been altered!

Calling ioctl() to re-read partition table.
Syncing disks.
#
```

To create a GPT partition table with **fdisk**, use the **g** option in **fdisk**. Next, type **n** to create a new partition. This example simply creates one large partition.

```
# fdisk /dev/sdc
Welcome to fdisk (util-linux 2.23.2).

Changes will remain in memory only, until you decide to
write them.
Be careful before using the write command.

Device does not contain a recognized partition table
Building a new DOS disklabel with disk identifier
0x774d7c12.

Command (m for help): g
Building a new GPT disklabel (GUID: B55798FB-5F51-42D1-
9E97-AAFA9074C0E4)


Command (m for help): n
Partition number (1-128, default 1):
First sector (2048-83886046, default 2048):
Last sector, +sectors or +size{K,M,G,T,P} (2048-83886046,
default 83886046):
Created partition 1


Command (m for help): p

Disk /dev/sdc: 42.9 GB, 42949672960 bytes, 83886080 sectors
Units = sectors of 1 * 512 = 512 bytes
Sector size (logical/physical): 512 bytes / 512 bytes
I/O size (minimum/optimal): 512 bytes / 512 bytes
```

```
Disk label type: gpt


#          Start        End    Size  Type              Name
1           2048   83886046    40G   Linux filesyste

Command (m for help): w
The partition table has been altered!

Calling ioctl() to re-read partition table.
Syncing disks.
```

Creating Filesystems

Before a partition can be used by a Linux system, it will need a filesystem. The extended file system, or ext for short, was created specifically for Linux. It was soon replaced with ext2, the second extended file system. Since then, ext3 (the third extended file system) and ext4 (the fourth extended file system) have been released. These are the most commonly used file systems on Linux systems and are often found as the default file systems on Linux distributions. If you have special needs, you should research some of the other popular filesystems available on Linux. These include ReiserFS, JFS, XFS, ZFS, and Btrfs.

To create a filesystem, use the **mkfs** command. The format is **mkfs -t TYPE DEVICE**. The **TYPE** will be a file system type such as ext3, btrfs, etc. The **DEVICE** is the path to the partition on which you want the file system to reside. Here is how to create an ext3 file system on the second partition of the **sdb** disk (/dev/sdb2).

```
# mkfs -t ext3 /dev/sdb2
mke2fs 1.42.9 (28-Dec-2013)
Filesystem label=
OS type: Linux
Block size=4096 (log=2)
Fragment size=4096 (log=2)
Stride=0 blocks, Stripe width=0 blocks
1310720 inodes, 5242880 blocks
262144 blocks (5.00%) reserved for the super user
First data block=0
```

31

```
Maximum filesystem blocks=4294967296
160 block groups
32768 blocks per group, 32768 fragments per group
8192 inodes per group
Superblock backups stored on blocks:
        32768, 98304, 163840, 229376, 294912, 819200,
884736, 1605632, 2654208,
        4096000

Allocating group tables: done
Writing inode tables: done
Creating journal (32768 blocks): done
Writing superblocks and filesystem accounting information:
done

#
```

Here is how to create an ext4 file system.

```
# mkfs -t ext4 /dev/sdb3
mke2fs 1.42.9 (28-Dec-2013)
Filesystem label=
OS type: Linux
Block size=4096 (log=2)
Fragment size=4096 (log=2)
Stride=0 blocks, Stripe width=0 blocks
32178176 inodes, 128712448 blocks
6435622 blocks (5.00%) reserved for the super user
First data block=0
Maximum filesystem blocks=2277507072
3928 block groups
32768 blocks per group, 32768 fragments per group
8192 inodes per group
Superblock backups stored on blocks:
        32768, 98304, 163840, 229376, 294912, 819200,
884736, 1605632, 2654208,
        4096000, 7962624, 11239424, 20480000, 23887872,
71663616, 78675968,
        102400000

Allocating group tables: done
Writing inode tables: done
Creating journal (32768 blocks): done
Writing superblocks and filesystem accounting information:
done
#
```

The **mkfs** utility is actually a front-end for the various file system builders. Running **mkfs -t ext4 /dev/sdb3** is actually the same as running **mkfs.ext4 /dev/sdb3**. If you want to see the options available for a specific file system, consult the man page for the given command. For example, you can run **man mkfs.xfs** to find more information about creating XFS file systems.

```
# ls -1 /sbin/mkfs*
/sbin/mkfs
/sbin/mkfs.btrfs
/sbin/mkfs.cramfs
/sbin/mkfs.ext2
/sbin/mkfs.ext3
/sbin/mkfs.ext4
/sbin/mkfs.minix
/sbin/mkfs.xfs
#
```

Mounting and Unmounting Partitions

To mount a partition, use the **mount** command followed by the path to the device and then the directory where you want to mount that device. For example, to mount /dev/sdb3 on /opt, run **mount /dev/sdb3 /opt**.

```
# mount /dev/sdb3 /opt
#
```

You can use the mount command without any arguments to see what is currently mounted. Be aware that mount will not only show physical filesystems but also virtual filesystems. These virtual filesystems are often RAM based filesystems that provide ways to interact with other parts of the system. If you want a shorter list of mount points that contain storage devices, use the **df** command. You can think of the **df** command as the "disk-free" command, as it reports file system usage.

```
# mount
proc on /proc type proc (rw,nosuid,nodev,noexec,relatime)
sysfs on /sys type sysfs (rw,nosuid,nodev,noexec,relatime)
devtmpfs on /dev type devtmpfs
(rw,nosuid,size=500196k,nr_inodes=125049,mode=755)
securityfs on /sys/kernel/security type securityfs
```

```
(rw,nosuid,nodev,noexec,relatime)
tmpfs on /dev/shm type tmpfs (rw,nosuid,nodev)
devpts on /dev/pts type devpts
(rw,nosuid,noexec,relatime,gid=5,mode=620,ptmxmode=000)
tmpfs on /run type tmpfs (rw,nosuid,nodev,mode=755)
tmpfs on /sys/fs/cgroup type tmpfs
(rw,nosuid,nodev,noexec,mode=755)
cgroup on /sys/fs/cgroup/systemd type cgroup
(rw,nosuid,nodev,noexec,relatime,xattr,release_agent=/usr/l
ib/systemd/systemd-cgroups-agent,name=systemd)
pstore on /sys/fs/pstore type pstore
(rw,nosuid,nodev,noexec,relatime)
cgroup on /sys/fs/cgroup/cpuset type cgroup
(rw,nosuid,nodev,noexec,relatime,cpuset)
cgroup on /sys/fs/cgroup/cpu,cpuacct type cgroup
(rw,nosuid,nodev,noexec,relatime,cpuacct,cpu)
cgroup on /sys/fs/cgroup/memory type cgroup
(rw,nosuid,nodev,noexec,relatime,memory)
cgroup on /sys/fs/cgroup/devices type cgroup
(rw,nosuid,nodev,noexec,relatime,devices)
cgroup on /sys/fs/cgroup/freezer type cgroup
(rw,nosuid,nodev,noexec,relatime,freezer)
cgroup on /sys/fs/cgroup/net_cls type cgroup
(rw,nosuid,nodev,noexec,relatime,net_cls)
cgroup on /sys/fs/cgroup/blkio type cgroup
(rw,nosuid,nodev,noexec,relatime,blkio)
cgroup on /sys/fs/cgroup/perf_event type cgroup
(rw,nosuid,nodev,noexec,relatime,perf_event)
cgroup on /sys/fs/cgroup/hugetlb type cgroup
(rw,nosuid,nodev,noexec,relatime,hugetlb)
configfs on /sys/kernel/config type configfs (rw,relatime)
/dev/sda2 on / type xfs (rw,relatime,attr2,inode64,noquota)
systemd-1 on /proc/sys/fs/binfmt_misc type autofs
(rw,relatime,fd=32,pgrp=1,timeout=300,minproto=5,maxproto=5
,direct)
debugfs on /sys/kernel/debug type debugfs (rw,relatime)
mqueue on /dev/mqueue type mqueue (rw,relatime)
hugetlbfs on /dev/hugepages type hugetlbfs (rw,relatime)
/dev/sdb3 on /opt type ext4 (rw,relatime,data=ordered)
# df -h
Filesystem      Size  Used Avail Use% Mounted on
/dev/sda2       198G  1.7G  196G   1% /
devtmpfs        489M     0  489M   0% /dev
tmpfs           497M     0  497M   0% /dev/shm
tmpfs           497M  6.5M  491M   2% /run
tmpfs           497M     0  497M   0% /sys/fs/cgroup
```

```
/dev/sdb3        484G   73M  459G   1% /opt
#
```

Note that manually mounting a file system from the command line will not cause it to persist between reboots. In order to make the mount permanent, you will need to add an entry in the **/etc/fstab** file. This will be covered in a later section of this book.

To unmount a partition, use the **umount** command followed by either the device path or the mount point. To unmount /opt, you could run **umount /opt** or **umount /dev/sdb3**.

```
# umount /opt
# df
Filesystem      1K-blocks     Used Available Use% Mounted on
/dev/sda2       206747000 1766844 204980156   1% /
devtmpfs           500196        0    500196   0% /dev
tmpfs              508740        0    508740   0% /dev/shm
tmpfs              508740     6612    502128   2% /run
tmpfs              508740        0    508740   0%
/sys/fs/cgroup
#
```

Creating Swap Space

Instead of creating a file system and mounting it, with swap you create a swap area and enable it. To prepare the swap partition for use, use the **mkswap** command followed by the path to the partition. To enable the swap partition, use the **swapon** command followed by the path to the device. To see the swap devices in use, run **swapon -s**.

```
# mkswap /dev/sdb1
Setting up swapspace version 1, size = 1048572 KiB
no label, UUID=619dc6d9-1b0b-4a9a-9df5-bfc343fb8d6e
# swapon /dev/sdb1
# swapon -s
Filename                               Type
Size     Used    Priority
/dev/sda1                              partition
2047996 0        -1
/dev/sdb1                              partition
1048572 0        -2
```

The File System Table

The **/etc/fstab** file controls where devices are mounted on a Linux system and what options to use when mounting those devices. Each entry consists of one line with six columns. If a line starts with **#**, it's a comment and is ignored. The six columns are the device, mount point, filesystem type, options, dump, and file system check order. Each of these columns is separated by a space or a tab. Here is an example **/etc/fstab** file.

```
# device   mount point   filesystem   options     dump  fsck

/dev/sda2 /              xfs          defaults     0     1
/dev/sda1 swap           swap         defaults     0     0
```

Device

This column contains a path to a device, a label for a device, or a UUID (universally unique identifier) of a device.

Mount Point

This column determines where the device will be mounted.

Filesystem Type

The third column contains the filesystem type. Use the same type here are as you did when you created the filesystem with the **mkfs** command.

Mount Options

Use this column to specify which options to mount the filesystem with. The keyword **defaults** represents the defaults for the filesystem which are typically the rw, suid, dev, exec, auto, nouser, and async options. Consult the man page for fstab, mount, and the filesystem for a full list of options. To specify multiple options separate them with a comma. Do not use spaces before or after the commas.

Dump

This column is used by **dump** utility. If it contains a 0, dump will ignore this filesystem. If it contains a 1, dump will backup this filesystem. You can safely ignore this column if you do not use the **dump** utility to perform backups. Today, **dump** is rarely used for backups.

Fsck

This column is used by the **fsck** program at boot time to determine if a filesystem is to be checked and in what order to check the filesystems. Valid values are 0, 1, and 2.   If this column contains a 0, **fsck** will skip checking this filesystem. File systems with a value of 1 will be checked first then the filesystems with a value of 2 will be checked next. For filesystems that you want to have checked, it's a best practice to set the **/** filesystem to 1 with the remaining filesystems set to 2.

Let's look at the example **/etc/fstab** file again.

```
# device  mount point  filesystem  options    dump  fsck

/dev/sda2 /            xfs         defaults   0     1
/dev/sda1 swap         swap        defaults   0     0
```

The first entry ensures that **/dev/sda2** will get mounted on **/**. Its filesytem type is xfs and it uses the default options. Since the dump column contains a 0, the dump utility will not backup this filesystem. The value in the fsck column is 1, so this filesystem will get checked first during the boot up.

The second entry ensures that **/dev/sda1** will be used as a swap device. For swap devices, use the **swap** keyword as the mount point and filesystem type. The dump and fsck columns are set to 0 as swap space does not need to be backed up or checked.

This fstab uses UUIDs ands labels in the device column. The device with the UUID of dbae4fe7-b06f-4319-85dc-b93ba4a16b17 will be mounted on **/**. The device with the label **opt** will be mounted on /opt and the **/dev/sda1** device will be used as swap space.

```
UUID=dbae4fe7-b06f-4319-85dc-b93ba4a16b17 / xfs defaults
  0 1
LABEL=opt /opt           ext4          defaults 1 1
/dev/sda1 swap           swap          defaults   0      0
```

To view labels and UUIDs, use the **lsblk –f** command. If you are only interested in the UUIDs, you can use the **blkid** command.

```
# lsblk -f
 NAME    FSTYPE LABEL UUID
MOUNTPOINT
sda
├─sda1 swap           1cb76bec-a1fa-4ac6-8296-c508e936b744
[SWAP]
└─sda2 xfs            dbae4fe7-b06f-4319-85dc-b93ba4a16b17 /
sdb
├─sdb1 swap           619dc6d9-1b0b-4a9a-9df5-bfc343fb8d6e
[SWAP]
├─sdb2 ext3           6517c68b-3671-42e7-9f37-e2fb9a549322
└─sdb3 ext4     opt   8b885f83-0d2c-4fe5-a4f1-dc678a9dec5a
sdc
└─sdc1
sr0
# blkid
/dev/sda1: UUID="1cb76bec-a1fa-4ac6-8296-c508e936b744"
TYPE="swap"
/dev/sda2: UUID="dbae4fe7-b06f-4319-85dc-b93ba4a16b17"
TYPE="xfs"
/dev/sdb1: UUID="619dc6d9-1b0b-4a9a-9df5-bfc343fb8d6e"
TYPE="swap"
/dev/sdb2: UUID="6517c68b-3671-42e7-9f37-e2fb9a549322"
SEC_TYPE="ext2" TYPE="ext3"
/dev/sdb3: LABEL="opt" UUID="8b885f83-0d2c-4fe5-a4f1-
dc678a9dec5a" TYPE="ext4"
```

Each filesystem type will have a utility that you can use to create or modify the label for the filesystem. For ext filesystems, you can use the **e2label** command. Simply pass the path to the device as the first argument and the label as the second argument. Here is how to add the label "opt" to the **/dev/sdb3** device.

```
# e2label /dev/sdb3 opt
```

Summary

In this chapter, you learned what partition tables are and some of the reasons to use partitions. You also learned about the GPT and MBR partition tables. This chapter covered mount points and how they are simply directories that are used to access the data on a partition. You also learned how to create partitions using the **fdisk** utility.

Creating file systems with the **mkfs** command was covered as well as how to mount those file systems with the **mount** command. Once a file system is mounted you learned how to view the disk usage with the **df** command. Next, we talked about using the **umount** command to unmount file systems. You also learned how to prepare swap space using the **mkswp** command and how to enable it with **swapon**.

Quiz

1. Partitioning a disk allows you to allocate different sections of the disk for different purposes.

    a. True

    b. False

2. How many primary partitions does the MBR partitioning scheme allow?

    a. 2

    b. 3

    c. 4

    d. Unlimited

3. A mount point is simply a directory that is used to access data on a partition.

    a. True

    b. False

4. These two commands perform the same task:

   mkfs -t ext4 /dev/sdb3

   mkfs.ext4 /dev/sdb3

    a. True

    b. False

5. Which command is used to unmount a filesystem.

    a. unmount

    b. umount

    c. dismount

6. The /etc/filetab file controls where devices are mounted on a Linux system and what options to use when mounting those devices.

    a. True

    b. False

7. Which command or commands can be used to view a UUID?

    a. Only the uuid command.

    b. Only the lsblk command.

    c. Only the blkid command.

    d. Both the lsblk and blkid commands.

8. What command prepares a swap partition for use. Afterwards, you can enable the swap partition with the **swapon** command.

    a. mkswap

    b. mkswp

    c. makeswap

Quiz Answers

1. A

2. C

3. A

4. A

5. B

6. B

7. D

8. A

Managing Users and Groups

Linux is a multi-user operating system. Not only can multiple accounts exist on the system, but each of those accounts can be used at the same time. Each account consists of a username and a unique number called the UID, short for user ID. Also, each account has a default group to which it belongs, some comments associated with the account, a shell to execute when the user logs into the system, and a home directory. All this information is stored in the **/etc/passwd** file.

The first entry in the **/etc/passwd** file is the **root** account.

```
root:x:0:0:root:/root:/bin/bash
```

The format of the **/etc/passwd** file is as follows.

```
username:password:UID:GID:comments:home_dir:shell
```

Each field is separated by a colon. Let's take a look at each of them individually.

Username: root

Password: x (This means the encrypted password is stored in **/etc/shadow** which you will learn about shortly.)
UID: 0
GID: 0
Comment: root
Home directory: /root
Shell: /bin/bash

Let's look at another entry in the **/etc/passwd** file. This is for the **joe** account.

```
joe:x:1000:1000:Joe Henderson:/home/joe:/bin/bash
```

Username: joe
Password: x
UID: 1000
GID: 1000
Comment: Joe Henderson
Home directory: /home/joe
Shell: /bin/bash

Even though Linux supports usernames up to 32 characters in length, it is customary to keep usernames to 8 or fewer characters. When using usernames longer than 8 characters, you will see run into situations where the UID is displayed in place of the username or a truncated version of the username is displayed. For example, when looking at output from the **ps** command.

Here is an example of a long username being truncated.

```
# ps -fu jasoncannon
UID         PID  PPID  C STIME TTY          TIME CMD
jasonca+   2973     1  0 01:43 ?        00:00:00 bash
```

This is what it might look like on an older version of Linux. The long username is simply replaced by it's UID.

```
# ps -fu jasoncannon
```

```
UID          PID  PPID  C STIME TTY          TIME CMD
1000         2973    1  0 01:43 ?        00:00:00 bash
```

Usernames are case sensitive. Even though uppercase letters are allowed in usersnames, by convention usernames are in all lower case letters. Digits are also allowed in usernames, but avoid special characters.

Historically, encrypted password information was stored in the **/etc/passwd** file following the username. However the **/etc/passwd** file is readable by anyone on the system so storing password information, even encrypted, is a security risk. Now, by default, the encrypted password information is stored in **/etc/shadow** which is readable only by the superuser account.

The UID is a unique number. The root account is always UID 0. Accounts meant to be used by the system typically have UIDs lower than 1000. This is configurable by updating the **/etc/login.defs** file.

The group ID, or GID, listed in the password file entry for an account is the account's default group. When a user creates a file that file will belong to the user's default group. If a user wants to create files using another group, they can use the **newgrp** command to change to a new group before creating the files.

The comment field typically contains the user's real name or a description of what the account is used for. It can also remain empty. You'll sometimes hear this field refered to as the GECOS field. This is a historical hold over from the early years of Unix.

When a user logs into the system they are placed in their home directory, listed in the **passwd** file. If this directory does not exist, they will be placed into the root directory.

The shell will be executed when the user logs into the system with their account. You can see a list of installed shells on your Linux system by looking at **/etc/shells**. Whatever is listed in the shell field will be executed upon login even if the program is not actually a shell. For example, you may see **/usr/sbin/nologin** or **/bin/false** in the shell field for certain accounts. This ensures that no one can use those accounts interactively. You can also use the shell field to execute a program when a user logs into the system. For example, you could force users into a menu driven application that only allows them access to certain actions.

The Shadow File

Like the **/etc/passwd** file, the **/etc/shadow** file contains a series of fields separated by a colon.

```
root:$6$9g1IC8AYzqPorEZSHjWeZP8o21:16502:0:99999:7:::
```

The first field is the username. The second field contains the encrypted password. The third field is the number of days since January 1, 1970 since the password has been changed. The fourth field is the number of days before the password can be changed. The fifth field is the number of days after which the password must be changed. If this field contains 99999 the user never has to change their password. The sixth field is the number of days at which to warn the user that their password will expire. The seventh field is the number of days after the password expires that the account is disabled. The eighth field is the number of days since Janary 1, 1970 that an account has been disabled. The ninth field is reserved for future use.

Creating Accounts

Now that you know where account information is stored, let's create an account using the **useradd** command. Adding accounts requires superuser privileges, so make sure you are using the root account or sudo. Here is the format of the **useradd** command.

```
useradd [options] username
```

The most commonly used options for the **useradd** command are:

`-c "COMMENT"` Comments for the account, such as the user's full name.

`-m`   Use the **-m** option to create the user's home directory.

`-s /shell/path` The path to the user's shell.

In this example, an account is created for Grant Stewart. His username is **grant** and his shell is **bash**.

```
# useradd -c "Grant Stewart" -m -s /bin/bash grant
```

Next, let's assign the account a password. To do this, use the **passwd** command followed by the username. You'll be prompted to enter a password for the user and then confirm that password.

```
# passwd grant
Enter new UNIX password:
Retype new UNIX password:
passwd: password updated successfully
```

Here is the entry for the account in the **/etc/passwd** file and **/etc/shadow** file.

```
# tail -1 /etc/passwd
grant:x:1000:1000:Grant Stewart:/home/grant:/bin/bash
# tail -1 /etc/shadow
grant:
$6$iDDgPYtR$0D1s0AMkFkQ7NvQe8c2Uc.:16507:0:99999:7:::
```

Grant's UID is **1000**, his GID is **1000**, his home directory is **/home/grant** and his shell is **/bin/bash**.

Other options for the **useradd** command include the following:

-g GROUP Specify the default group for the account.

-G GROUP1,GROUPN Add the account to additional groups.

Let's create an account for Eddie Harris. His login will be **eharris** and his default group will be **sales**. We will also make him a member of the **projectx** group as well.

```
# useradd -c "Eddie Harris" -m -s /bin/bash -g sales
-G projectx eharris
# passwd eharris
Enter new UNIX password:
Retype new UNIX password:
passwd: password updated successfully
#
```

Creating System or Application Accounts

Not every account on a Linux system is meant to be used by a person. Some accounts exist to run applications or perform system functions. Some common examples of this include accounts that run web server processes, database processes, or application processes.

Let's create an account that will be used to run the Apache web server process.

```
# useradd -c "Apache Web Server User" -d /opt/apache
-r -s /usr/sbin/nologin apache
# tail -1 /etc/passwd
apache:x:999:999:Apache Web Server
User:/opt/apache:/usr/sbin/nologin
#
```

You'll notice that the shell was set to **/usr/sbin/nologin**. This is because we don't want someone to be able to log into the system using the account. We also use the **-r** option, which instructs **useradd** to create a system account. Effectivly, this means the account will receive a UID in the system account range as defined in **/etc/login.defs**. In this instance the user received UID **999**.

The home directory was specified using the **-d** option. By default, the home directory for a new account is created in the **/home** directory. The actual directory will be the name of the user account. By default, the **apache** account's home directory will be **/home/apache**. However, since this account will be used by an application, we set the home directory to the directory where the application is installed.

Notice that the **-m** option was not used in this instance. When using the **-m** option the contents of the skeleton directory, **/etc/skel** by default, are copied into the user's home directory. The contents of **/etc/skel** usually include shell configuration files which are not needed for application accounts.

Here are the new options we used to create this account.

-r   Create a system account.

-d /path/to/home   Use **-d** to specify a home directory.

It's a common practice to use the same **UID** for an account across multiple sytems. This makes syncing data or sharing data easier to do as Linux uses UID's to determine a file's ownership. The account name is really for the sake of us humans. Let's use the **-u** option to specify a UID when creating an account.

```
# useradd -c "MySQL Server" -d /opt/mysql -u 97 -s
/usr/sbin/nologin mysql
# tail -1 /etc/passwd
mysql:x:97:1003:MySQL
Server:/opt/mysql:/usr/sbin/nologin
#
```

-u UID   Specify the numeric UID for the user.

Deleting Accounts

To delete an account, use the **userdel** command followed by the username. If you want to delete the account's home directory use the -r option. It also removes the users mail spool if it exists.

In the example, we'll delete the **eharris** account, but leave his home directory intact since there are some files in there we want to use later. We'll also delete the **grant** account and remove his home directory.

```
# ls /home
eharris grant
# userdel eharris
# ls /home
eharris grant
# userdel -r grant
# ls /home
eharris
#
```

Updating Accounts

To update, or modify, an existing account, use the **usermod** command. Here are the most commonly used options to the **usermod** command. For a full listing of all the options available see **man usermod** or **usermod --help**.

usermod [options] username

-c "COMMENT" Update the comment field.

-g GROUP Change the primary group.

-G GROUP1,GROUPN Change the additional groups the account belongs to.

-s /path/to/shell Change the account's shell.

In this example, we update the comment associated witht the **mysql** account.

```
# grep mysql /etc/passwd
mysql:x:97:1003:MySQL
Server:/opt/mysql:/usr/sbin/nologin
# usermod -c "MySQL User" mysql
# grep mysql /etc/passwd
mysql:x:97:1003:MySQL
```

```
User:/opt/mysql:/usr/sbin/nologin
#
```

Groups

Group details are stored in the **/etc/group** file.

The first entry in the **/etc/group** file is the **root** group.

```
root:x:0:
```

Here is another sample entry from **/etc/group**.

```
sales:x:1001:john,mary
```

The format of the **/etc/group** file is as follows.

```
group_name:password:GID:account1,accountN
```

Each field is separated by a colon. The group name is the human readable name that you will see when group information is displayed by commands such as **ls**.

The password is used for privileged groups, but that functionality is rarely used. When there is an **x** in this field it means that shadow group passwords are being used. That information is stored in the **/etc/gshadow** file.

The GID is the group ID. It is simply a unique number which represents the group.

The remaining field lists the members of the group separated by commas.

You might have noticed that the root group did not contain a list of members. Remember that the **/etc/passwd** file specifies an account's default group. In the case of the root user, the default GID is 0. When an account's default GID is listed in the **/etc/passwd** file, that account is in that group even if it is not listed in the members field in the

/etc/group file.

```
# grep root /etc/passwd
root:x:0:0:root:/root:/bin/bash
# grep root /etc/group
root:x:0:
```

To display the groups that a member belongs to, pass the username to the **groups** command. If you execute the **groups** command without supplying a username, your group memberships will be listed.

groups [options] [username]

Let's confirm that the root user is in fact in the root group.

```
# groups root
root
```

Creating Groups

To create a group, use the **groupadd** command.

```
groupadd [options] group
```

-g GID Assign the numerical value for the group ID.

The most commonly used option for the **groupadd** command is **-g**, which allows you to specify the GID. Let's create two groups. For the first group, we'll let the group command automatically select the GID. For the second group, we'll specify the GID.

```
# groupadd web
# tail -1 /etc/group
web:x:1003:
# groupadd -g 2500 db
# tail -1 /etc/group
db:x:2500:
#
```

Deleting Groups

To delete a group, simply pass the group name to the **groupdel** command.

```
groupdel group
```

Let's delete the **db** group.

```
# groupdel db
#
```

Updating Groups

To change the properties of an existing group, use the **groupmod** command.

```
groupmod [options] group
```

-g GID Change the group ID to GID.

-n GROUP   Change the name of the group to GROUP.

In this example, we changed the GID of the web group from 1003 to 1234. Next we'll change the name from web to http.

```
# grep web /etc/group
web:x:1003:
# groupmod -g 1234 web
# grep web /etc/group
web:x:1234:
# groupmod -n http web
# grep http /etc/group
http:x:1234:
```

Putting Groups and Users Together

In the following example, we are going to create a **writers** group, a **tv** group, and a **movie** group. Next we are going to create some user accounts. All of these user accounts will belong to the **writers** groups, but only some of them will belong to the **tv** group, while the others will belong to the **movie** group.

```
# groupadd writers
# groupadd tv
# groupadd movie
# useradd -c "Carlton Cuse" -g writers -G tv -m -s
/bin/bash ccuse
# passwd ccuse
Enter new UNIX password:
Retype new UNIX password:
passwd: password updated successfully
# groups ccuse
ccuse : writers tv
# useradd -c "David Fury" -g writers -G tv -m -s
/bin/bash dfury
# passwd dfury
Enter new UNIX password:
Retype new UNIX password:
passwd: password updated successfully
# groups dfury
dfury : writers tv
# useradd -c "Matt Damon" -g writers -G movie -m -s
/bin/bash mdamon
# passwd mdamon
Enter new UNIX password:
Retype new UNIX password:
passwd: password updated successfully
# groups mdamon
mdamon : writers movie
# useradd -c "Ben Affleck" -g writers -G movie -m -s
/bin/bash baffleck
# passwd mdamon
Enter new UNIX password:
Retype new UNIX password:
passwd: password updated successfully
# groups baffleck
baffleck : writers movie
# tail -3 /etc/group
writers:x:1235:
tv:x:1236:ccuse,dfury
```

```
movie:x:1237:mdamon,baffleck
# grep 1235 /etc/passwd
ccuse:x:1000:1235:Carlton Cuse:/home/ccuse:/bin/bash
dfury:x:1001:1235:David Fury:/home/dfury:/bin/bash
mdamon:x:1002:1235:Matt Damon:/home/mdamon:/bin/bash
baffleck:x:1003:1235:Ben
Affleck:/home/baffleck:/bin/bash
#
```

Summary

Account information is stored in the **/etc/passwd** and **/etc/shadow** files. In addition to a username, each account consists of a unique number called the UID, a default group, a comment, a home directory location, and a login shell.

Accounts can be created with the **useradd** command. To delete an account, use the **userdel** command. To modify an account, use the **usermod** command.

Group information is stored in the **/etc/group** file. To create a group, use the **groupadd** command. You can delete groups by using the **groupdel** command. To update an existing group use the **groupmod** command. To list group memberships for an account, use the **groups** command.

Quiz

1. Which file stores account information?

    a. /etc/accounts

    b. /etc/passwordfile

    c. /etc/password

    d. /etc/passwd

2. The /etc/shadow file stores encrypted passwords.

    a. True

    b. False

3. What UID is always assigned to the root account?

    a. 0

    b. 1

    c. 100

    d. 1000

4. What command displays the group memberships for a user?

    a. groupshow

    b. lsgroups

    c. listgroups

    d. groups

5. What file stores group information?

    a. /etc/groups

    b. /etc/group

    c. /etc/memberships

6. The **sudo** command allows users to run processes as other users, most typically the root user.

    a. True

    b. False

7. Which command is used to set or change passwords for Linux accounts?

    a. password

    b. pwd

    c. passwd

    d. pswd

Quiz Answers

1. D

2. A

3. A

4. D

5. B

6. A

7. C

Networking

In this chapter, you will learn about the TCP/IP protocol and the most important aspects of IP networking. You'll also be introduced to network classes and classful networks. Additionally, you'll be learning about subnet masks and broadcast addresses. Next you'll learn about classless interdomain routing and, finally, you'll learn what IP addresses are meant to be used on private networks.

Today, TCP/IP is the de facto standard for transmitting data over networks. TCP/IP stands for Transmission Control Protocol (TCP) and Internet Protocol (IP). TCP is responsible for establishing and maintaining network conversations so that two devices can exchange data. The Internet Protocol is responsible for sending data from one device to another device on a network. Each one of these network devices is known as a host and has at least one IP address.

For a device on a network to communicate properly, it needs three pieces of information: an IP address, a subnet mask, and a broadcast address. Each one of these numbers is comprised of four octets separated by a dot. An octet represents eight-bits and therefore can have a value starting at 0 and going up to 255.

Example IP Address: 199.83.131.168

Example Subnet Mask: 255.255.255.0

Example Broadcast Address: 199.83.131.255

In the example IP Address of 199.83.131.186, the first octet contains a value of 199, the second octet is 83, the third octet is 131, and the last octet is 186.

IP addresses are comprised of two parts. The first part of an IP address is the network address and the second part is the host address. The network portion of the IP address tells routers what network the host belongs to and thus where to route data that is destined for that host. The host address tells routers the specific device that the data should be sent to. For routing to work properly, each group of devices, or network, needs to have a unique network address. Also, each device within that network needs to have a unique host address.

The class of an address determines what portion is used as the network address and what portion is used for host addresses.

Class	Network	Hosts Allowed
A	1 -> 127 Ex: 17.24.88.9	16,777,216
B	128.0 -> 191.255 Ex: 183.194.46.31	65,536
C	192.0.0 -> 233.255.255 Ex: 199.83.131.186	255

By looking at the first octet of an IP address, you can tell what class it is. An IP address with a first octet that falls between 1 and 127 is a class A IP address. For example, the IP address 17.24.88.9 belongs to a class A network. Class B addresses begin with 128.0 and end at 191.255. For example, 183.194.46.31 belongs to a class B network. Class C addresses start with 192.0.0 and end with 233.255.255. An example IP address that belongs to a class C network is 199.83.131.186.

A class determines the possible number of networks and the addressable space per network. For example, a Class A network can accommodate about 16 million host addresses. A Class B network can have up to 65,536 hosts in it, and a class C network can address 255 hosts.

The following table lists the subnet mask used for each of the network classes. The network portion of an IP address corresponds to the 255s in the subnet mask. For example, the first octet of a Class A network is the network portion while the three remaining octets are the host portion. For Class B networks, the first two octets are for network addresses while the last two octets are for host addresses. Finally, Class C networks use the first three octets for the network and just the last octet for the host addresses.

Class	Subnet Mask
A	255.0.0.0
B	255.255.0.0
C	255.255.255.0

Let's take the IP address 183.194.46.31 as an example. That particular IP address is in a class B network since it falls in the range of 128.0 to 191.255. The network port of the address is 183.194 and the host portion is 46.31.

Netmask	255	255	0	0
IP Address	183	194	46	31

The netmask is listed right above the IP address so you can see how the network portion aligns with the 255 values and the host portion aligns with the 0 values.

A broadcast address is a special logical address used to send data to all hosts on a given network. In addition to their own IP addresses, all network hosts receive data sent to the broadcast address. You can quickly determine the broadcast IP address by using the value 255 in the octets where there are 0's in the subnet mask. The following table lists a few examples. For the class A network of 17.0.0.0 that uses a netmask of 255.0.0.0, the broadcast address is 17.255.255.255. The next two examples follow the same pattern as you might expect. The Class B network employs the default 255.255.0.0 subnet mask and the Class C network uses a 255.255.255.0 subnet mask.

Class	Network	Subnet Mask	Broadcast
A	17.0.0.0	255.0.0.0	17.255.255.255
B	183.194.0.0	255.255.0.0	183.194.255.255
C	199.83.131.0	255.255.255.0	199.83.131.255

Classless Inter-Domain Routing

CIDR stands for Classless Inter-Domain Routing. It allows networks to be subdivided regardless of their traditional class. These subdivided networks are called subnets. For example, the IP address 121.67.198.94 falls in the Class A network range. By default, the network is 121.0.0.0, the subnet mask is 255.0.0.0, and the broadcast address is 121.255.255.255. However, if you specify a subnet mask, you can alter the portion of the IP address that is used as the network and the portion that is used as the host address. By specifiying a 255.255.255.0 subnet with the 121.67.198.94 address, the network becomes 121.67.198.0 and the broadcast address becomes 121.67.198.255.

Reserved Private Address Space

There are ranges of IP addresses that are dedicated for use in private networks. You'll often see these types of IP addresses being used in your company's internal network and you'll most likely being using a range of these IP addresses for your home network as well.

These private addresses are also called non-routable IPs since they are not routed through the public Internet. You'll also hear these IP addresses referred to as RFC1918 address, which refers to the RFC1918 standards document where these private ranges were initially defined.

As you can see in the following table, there is a dedicated range of non-routable private address space for each network class. Keep in mind that you can subnet these networks however you like, regardless of their associated traditional class.

Class	Range	Private Address Space
A	1.0.0.0 - 127.255.255.255	10.0.0.0 - 10.255.255.255
B	128.0.0.0 - 191.255.255.255	172.16.0.0 - 172.31.255.255
C	192.0.0.0 - 233.255.255.255	192.168.0.0 - 192.168.255.255

Summary

In this chapter, you learned how the TCP/IP protocol is the defacto standard of transmitting data over a network. You also learned about Class A, B, and C networks. You learned about the default subnet masks and broadcast addresses used by the various network classes. You also learned that you can specify a subnet mask to divide larger networks into smaller ones called subnets. Finally, you learned what IP ranges are dedicated for use in private networks and how these IP address are not routed over the public Internet.

Quiz

1. 257.19.21.228 is a valid IP address.

   a. True

   b. False

2. Given an IP address of 199.83.131.0 and a subnet mask of 255.255.255.0, what is the broadcast address?

   a. 199.83.131.0

   b. 199.83.131.1

   c. 199.83.131.255

   d. 199.255.255.255

3. Which of the following IP addresses does not fall within a private address range?

   a. 10.11.12.13

   b. 11.12.13.14

   c. 172.16.255.255

   d. 192.168.1.100

Quiz Answers

1. B

2. C

3. B

Linux Networking

In this chapter, you'll learn how to configure and control the network interfaces on a Linux system as well as its hostname. You'll learn what DNS is and how to use the **host** and **dig** tools to resolve hostnames and IP addresses. You'll learn the roles that the /etc/hosts and /etc/nsswitch.conf files play in name resolution. You'll also be introduced to network ports. Next, you'll learn what DHCP is and how to configure your Linux system as a DHCP client. Finally, we'll look at menu driven tools that can assist you in managing the various network settings on the most popular Linux distributions.

To show your current IP address, or to get a list of all the IP addresses in use on your system, run the **ip** command with an argument of **address**. With the **ip** command, you can use abbreviations, so instead of running **ip address** you can run **ip addr** or even **ip a**. You can also be more explicit by running **ip address show**.

The following is some sample output from the **ip address** command. You can see two devices listed: lo and eth0. The lo device is the loopback device. This is a special virtual network interface that a Linux system uses to communicate with itself. The loopback device has an IP

address of 127.0.0.1. The other network device on this system is the
eth0 device. This is an actual hardware device and it has an ip address
of 192.168.1.122.

```
# ip address
1: lo: <LOOPBACK,UP,LOWER_UP> mtu 65536 qdisc noqueue
state UNKNOWN
    link/loopback 00:00:00:00:00:00 brd
00:00:00:00:00:00
    inet 127.0.0.1/8 scope host lo
       valid_lft forever preferred_lft forever
    inet6 ::1/128 scope host
       valid_lft forever preferred_lft forever
2: eth0: <BROADCAST,MULTICAST,UP,LOWER_UP> mtu 1500
qdisc pfifo_fast state UP qlen 1000
    link/ether 08:00:27:43:f5:18 brd
ff:ff:ff:ff:ff:ff
    inet 192.168.1.122/24 brd 192.168.1.255 scope
global dynamic eth0
       valid_lft 84249sec preferred_lft 84249sec
    inet6 fe80::a00:27ff:fe43:f518/64 scope link
       valid_lft forever preferred_lft forever
```

In addition to the **ip** command, the **ifconfig** tool can be used to display
IP address information. At this point the **ifconfig** utility is considered to
be deprecated. However, this little utility hasn't quite yet disappeared
on modern Linux systems and may be around for quite some time to
come. If this is a refresher for you or if you are coming from a Unix
background, you may already be familiar with the **ifconfig** command,
but not its newer replacement, the **ip** command. In this chapter, you
will learn how to use both the **ip** and **ifconfig** commands.

To display the ip address in use with the **ifconfig** command, execute it
without any arguments. Here is some output from the ifconfig
command. It lists two interfaces: eth0 and the loopback device. You'll
notice that the output is slightly different from the **ip** command.
However, it gets the job done by displaying the IP address, netmask, and

more. Just like with the **ip** command, you can see that the eth0 device has an IP of 192.168.1.122 and the loopback device has an IP of 127.0.0.1.

```
# ifconfig
eth0: flags=4163<UP,BROADCAST,RUNNING,MULTICAST>  mtu
1500
        inet 192.168.1.122  netmask 255.255.255.0
broadcast 192.168.1.255
        inet6 fe80::a00:27ff:fe43:f518  prefixlen 64
scopeid 0x20<link>
        ether 08:00:27:43:f5:18  txqueuelen 1000
(Ethernet)
        RX packets 82371  bytes 95773879 (91.3 MiB)
        RX errors 0  dropped 0  overruns 0  frame 0
        TX packets 32907  bytes 3386585 (3.2 MiB)
        TX errors 0  dropped 0 overruns 0  carrier 0
collisions 0

lo: flags=73<UP,LOOPBACK,RUNNING>  mtu 65536
        inet 127.0.0.1  netmask 255.0.0.0
        inet6 addr: ::1/128 Scope:Host
        UP LOOPBACK RUNNING  MTU:65536  Metric:1
        RX packets:250935 errors:0 dropped:0
overruns:0 frame:0
        TX packets:250935 errors:0 dropped:0
overruns:0 carrier:0
        collisions:0 txqueuelen:0
        RX bytes:70966872 (70.9 MB)  TX
bytes:70966872 (70.9 MB)
```

Hostnames

A host is a device connected to a network. Since we are talking about TCP/IP networking, a host in this case is a device with an IP address.

A hostname is simply a human-readable name that corresponds to an IP address. Let's say we have a Linux server that will act as a web server in production. We can give that server a hostname, webprod01 for example, and refer to it by that hostname instead of its IP address, which might be something like 10.109.155.174. A one word hostname like this is sometimes called the short hostname or the unqualified hostname.

DNS Hostnames

The primary purpose of DNS, which stands for Domain Name System, is to translate human readable names into IP addresses. Of course, DNS does the reverse as well. It can translate an IP address to a hostname.

The fully qualified domain name, or FQDN, of a host also contains a domain name and a top-level domain name. Each section of the FQDN is separated by a period.

TLD stands for top-level domain and is the rightmost portion of a DNS name. Common top level domains include .com, .net, and .org, but there actually hundreds of other top level domains.

A domain appears just to the left of a top-level domain. This is often a company name, an organization name, or a brand name.

The FQDN, or long hostname, of our Linux server would contain at least three strings separated by periods. For example, its FQDN could be webprod01.mycompany.com.

However, domains can be further divided into sub-domains. Let's say "My Company" wants to use subdomains to identify where a server is located. It could use a country domain such as us.mycompany.com and maybe even a state subdomain, something like ny.us.mycompany.com. If our web server were in New York, its FQDN might actually be webprod01.ny.us.mycompany.com. Subdomains do not have to correspond to geographical regions; they can be anything the DNS administrator has configured.

You can display the current hostname by using the **hostname** command or by running **uname -n**. In the following example, the hostname is webprod01. If you want to display the FQDN, run **hostname -f**.

```
$ hostname
webprod01
$ uname -n
webprod01
$ hostname -f
webprod01.mycompany.com
```

You can also temporarily change the hostname of a system by supplying it as an argument to the **hostname** command. However, to make this persist between reboots, you'll need to update the hostname configuration. This configuration varies slightly from distribution to distribution. For Ubuntu and RedHat systems, edit the /etc/hostname file and place your desired hostname there. For earlier versions of RedHat, you can edit the /etc/sysconfig/network file and set the HOSTNAME variable to the desired value.

```
# hostname webprod01

# echo 'webprod01' > /etc/hostname

# vi /etc/sysconfig/network
    HOSTNAME=webprod01
```

Resolving DNS Names

If you want to lookup or resolve a DNS name or an IP address, you can use the **host** or **dig** tools. In their simplest forms, you specify the IP address or dns name you want to lookup as an argument to the command. Here is an example of using the **host** command.

```
$ host www.mycompany.com
webprod01.mycompany.com has address 1.2.1.6
$ host 1.2.1.6
6.1.2.1.in-addr.arpa domain name pointer
www.mycompany.com.
```

Here is an example using **dig**. Use the **-x** option to perform a reverse lookup.

```
$ dig www.mycompany.com

; <<>> DiG 9.9.4-RedHat-9.9.4-18.el7_1.1 <<>>
www.mycompany.com
;; global options: +cmd
;; Got answer:
;; ->>HEADER<<- opcode: QUERY, status: NOERROR, id:
22904
;; flags: qr rd ra; QUERY: 1, ANSWER: 1, AUTHORITY:
0, ADDITIONAL: 1

;; OPT PSEUDOSECTION:
; EDNS: version: 0, flags:; udp: 512
;; QUESTION SECTION:
;www.mycompany.com.              IN      A

;; ANSWER SECTION:
www.mycompany.com.    292    IN      A        1.2.1.6

;; Query time: 13 msec
;; SERVER: 10.0.2.3#53(10.0.2.3)
;; WHEN: Wed Jan 13 03:30:17 JST 2016
;; MSG SIZE  rcvd: 62
$ dig -x 1.2.1.6
; <<>> DiG 9.9.4-RedHat-9.9.4-18.el7_1.1 <<>> -x
52.5.196.34
;; global options: +cmd
;; Got answer:
;; ->>HEADER<<- opcode: QUERY, status: NOERROR, id:
23203
;; flags: qr rd ra; QUERY: 1, ANSWER: 1, AUTHORITY:
0, ADDITIONAL: 1

;; OPT PSEUDOSECTION:
; EDNS: version: 0, flags:; udp: 512
;; QUESTION SECTION:
;6.1.2.1.in-addr.arpa.       IN    PTR
```

```
;; ANSWER SECTION:
6.1.2.1.in-addr.arpa. 299  IN   PTR www.mycompany.com
;; Query time: 34 msec
;; SERVER: 10.0.2.3#53(10.0.2.3)
;; WHEN: Wed Jan 13 03:33:16 JST 2016
;; MSG SIZE  rcvd: 106
$
```

The Hosts File

The /etc/hosts file contains a list of IP addresses and hostnames. You can create entries in the hosts file by starting a line with an IP address and then following it with the name or names you want to translate that IP address to. The following example entry uses multiple names, but if you don't need or want to access the system by multiple names, you can simply list one name. This entry could be one of many in the hosts file.

```
10.11.12.13 webprod02.mycorp.com webprod02
```

After you have created an entry in /etc/hosts, you can start communicating with that IP address by using the name listed in the host file. This can be useful if you want to access computers that do not have DNS hostnames. Also, it's common to use /etc/host entries to override the DNS entry of a system. For example, if you have a cluster of web servers you could have a private network that only the web cluster members can access. You can create an entry for the members of the cluster in /etc/hosts and use their private address, thus forcing network communications through the private network.

It's important to note that /etc/hosts is local to the system. Adding an entry to the /etc/hosts file does not add an entry into DNS.

Here is an example /etc/hosts file. You'll see the first line contains an entry for localhost. Remember that this is used by the loopback device for internal communications. The next line contains the public IP address of the system followed by the FQDN and then the short name. The third line contains a non-routable IP address for webprod02. In this example, it's the private IP address of that system. There is another similar entry for webprod03 on the next line. The last line is only contains one name: dbcluster.

```
127.0.0.1       localhost
1.2.1.6         webprod01.mycompany.com webprod01
10.11.12.14     webprod02.mycompany.com webprod02
10.11.12.15     webprod03.mycompany.com webprod03
10.11.13.7      dbcluster
```

Name Service Switch

Typically, the /etc/hosts file is checked first before a DNS server is queried, but you can change this behavior by editing the /etc/nsswitch.conf file. NSS stands for Name Service Switch and it controls the order in which lookups are performed.

The hosts line determines the order for name resolution. For example, if you have **hosts: files dns** in the nsswitch.conf file, the /etc/hosts file will be searched first. If an IP address is found, that IP is used and the search stops. If it is not found, then DNS is queried.

There are other services that can resolve hostnames. If you want to use NIS for name resolution you can add it to the hosts line in /etc/nsswitch.conf. Here is an example.

```
hosts: files nis dns
```

Here is an example /etc/nsswitch.conf file.

```
#
# /etc/nsswitch.conf
#
# An example Name Service Switch config file. This
# file should be sorted with the most-used services
# at the beginning.
```

```
#
# The entry '[NOTFOUND=return]' means that the search
# for an entry should stop if the search in the
# previous entry turned up nothing. Note that if the
# search failed due to some other reason(like no NIS
# server responding) then the search continues with
# the# next entry.
passwd:      files sss
shadow:      files sss
group:       files sss
hosts:       files dns myhostname
bootparams:  nisplus [NOTFOUND=return] files
ethers:      files
netmasks:    files
networks:    files
protocols:   files
rpc:         files
services:    files sss
netgroup:    files sss
publickey:   nisplus
automount:   files
aliases:     files nisplus
```

Network Ports

Just like IP addresses identify hosts on a network, ports identify the services on a host. When a service starts on a system, it binds itself to a port and listens for traffic destined for its port.

Ports range from 1 to 65,535. Ports from 1 through 1,023 are called well-known ports or system ports. These ports are pre-assigned ports and are used for common system services. These ports are also called privileged ports since it requires superuser privileges to open these ports. Ports above 1,024 can be opened and used by normal users on a system and are called unprivileged ports.

The following is a very short list of common ports. For example, port 22 is reserved for SSH, 25 for SMTP, 80 for HTTP, 143 for IMAP, 389 for LDAP, and 443 for HTTPS. For a complete list of ports visit http://www.linuxtrainingacademy.com/ports.

Port	Service
22	SSH
25	SMTP
80	HTTP
143	IMAP
389	LDAP
443	HTTPS

When you type https://www.mybank.com into address bar of your web browser, your computer translates www.mybank.com into an IP address. Then, your web browser initiates a request to that IP address on port 443. The service—in this case a web server—will receive the traffic on port 443.

The /etc/services file translates human-readable names into port numbers. Here you'll find a list of predefined ports. You can also add to this list. For instance, when you install third party software, you may need to add an entry in /etc/services for the service that software provides. You can also create entries for your own custom written applications that use ports.

Here is what the ports from the previous table would look like in the /etc/services file.

```
ssh     22/tcp    # SSH Remote Login Protocol
smtp    25/tcp    # SMTP
```

```
https   80/tcp   # HTTP
imap2   143/udp  # IMAP
ldap    389/tcp  # LDAP
https   443/tcp  # HTTP protocol over TLS/SSL
```

DHCP

DHCP stands for Dynamic Host Configuration Protocol. DHCP is primarily used to assign IP addresses to hosts on a network. When a DHCP client wants to request an IP address it sends a broadcast message looking for a DHCP server. The DHCP server then responds to the client and provides it with an IP address and other additional information such as the netmask, gateway, and DNS servers to use for name resolution. The DHCP client configures itself with this information and begins to communicate on the network.

The IP address assigned to a DHCP client is leased from the DHCP server. The client will be able to use that IP address for the lease expiration time configured by the DHCP server. If the DHCP client wants to continue using the IP address beyond the lease expiration time, it must send a renewal request to the DHCP server. If no renewal is received by the DHCP server, it will place this IP back into the pool of available addresses.

To configure a RedHat based system as a DHCP client, edit the network device configuration file located in the /etc/sysconfig/network-scripts directory. The name of this file will be ifcfg-network-device-name. Depending on the system configuration and the underlying hardware, it might be ifcfg-eth0 or even something like ifcfg-enp5s2. To get a list of network devices on your system, run **ifconfig -a or ip link**.

Once you've identified the configuration file for the network device, set the BOOTPROTO variable to "dhcp."

```
# ip link
1: lo: <LOOPBACK,UP,LOWER_UP> mtu 65536 qdisc noqueue
state UNKNOWN mode DEFAULT
```

```
    link/loopback 00:00:00:00:00:00 brd
00:00:00:00:00:00
2: enp0s3: <BROADCAST,MULTICAST,UP,LOWER_UP> mtu 1500
qdisc pfifo_fast state UP mode DEFAULT qlen 1000
    link/ether 08:00:27:ba:8f:35 brd
ff:ff:ff:ff:ff:ff
# cat /etc/sysconfig/network-scripts/ifcfg-enp0s3
DEVICE="enp0s3"
ONBOOT=yes
NETBOOT=yes
IPV6INIT=yes
BOOTPROTO=dhcp
TYPE=Ethernet
NAME="enp0s3"
#
```

To configure an Ubuntu system as a DHCP client, edit the
/etc/network/interfaces file. Add the dhcp method to the inet address
family statement for the interface. The line will read **iface <network-
device-name> inet dhcp**. For eth0, this will be **iface eth0 inet dhcp**.
Here are the contents of an example /etc/network/interfaces file.

```
#/etc/network/interfaces
# This file describes the network interfaces
# available on your system and how to activate them.
# For more information, see interfaces(5).

# The loopback network interface
auto lo
iface lo inet loopback

# The primary network interface
auto eth0
iface eth0 inet dhcp
```

You can also assign a static IP address to a Linux system. For RedHat
based systems, edit the network interface configuration file located in
/etc/sysconfig/network-scripts. Be sure to set the BOOTPROTO variable

to static. Assign the IP address, netmask, network, broadcast, and gateway as shown in the following example. If you want the network device to be activated at boot time, set ONBOOT to yes.

```
DEVICE="enp0s3"
BOOTPROTO=static
IPADDR=10.109.155.174
NETMASK=255.255.255.0
NETWORK=10.109.155.0
BROADCAST=10.109.155.255
GATEWAY=10.109.155.1
ONBOOT=yes
```

To assign an interface a static IP address on an Ubuntu system, edit the /etc/network/interfaces file. Use the **static** keyword following **inet** on the **iface** line for the network interface. Next, supply the IP address, netmask, and gateway address.

```
 auto eth0
iface eth0 inet static
        address 10.109.155.174
        netmask 255.255.255.0
        gateway 10.109.155.1
```

You can use the **ip** command to manually assign an IP address to a network interface. The format is **ip address add IP[/NETMASK] dev NETWORK_DEVICE.** To add the IP address 10.11.12.13 to eth0, run **ip address add 10.11.12.13 dev eth0.** You can also supply the netmask by following the IP address with a forward slash and then providing the netmask like so: **ip address add 10.11.12.13/255.255.255.0 dev eth0.** To bring the interface up, **run ip link set eth0 up.**

If the ifconfig tool is available, you can use it to assign IP addresses to network interfaces as well. The format is **ifconfig NETWORK_DEVICE addr netmask SUBNET_MASK.** To add the IP address 10.11.12.13 to eth0 with **ifconfig**, run **ifconfig eth0 10.11.12.13.** To specify the netmask, use the netmask keyword and follow it by the netmask you intend to use. Run **ifconfig eth0 10.11.12.13 netmask 255.255.255.0,** for example. To bring the interface up, run **ifconfig eth0 up**.

An easier way to bring network interfaces up and down is by using the **ifup** and **ifdown** commands. These commands are actually scripts that are provided by many Linux distributions. They use the information specified in the network configuration files to configure the interfaces. If you make a configuration change you can test your change by using the **ifup** and **ifdown** commands. Here are a few examples.

```
#  ifup eth0
# ifup enp5s2
# ifdown eth0
# ifdown enp5s2
```

Instead of manually editing network configuration files, some distributions supply GUI or TUI tools. GUI stands for graphical user interface and TUI stands for textual user interface.

RedHat supplies a TUI called **nmtui**. You can run **nmtui** as root and use the simple menu driven interface to configure your network devices. Older versions of RedHat include a very similar utility called **system-config-network**. You can use YaST, which stands for Yet Another Setup Tool, on Suse systems. At the time of this writing, there are no official Ubuntu network configuration tools available.

Summary

In this chapter, you learned to see what IP addresses are assigned to the network interfaces on a Linux system. You also learned how to manually add IP addresses using the **ip** and **ifconfig** utilities. Next, you learned how to set and get the hostname of a system. We also talked about DNS and using the **host** and **dig** utilities to resolve names and IP addresses. You learned how to make entries in /etc/hosts and how to control the order in which name resolutions take place by using the /etc/nsswitch.conf file.

Network ports were covered and you learned how superuser privileges are required to open ports below 1,024. You also learned that the primary purpose of DHCP is to assign IP addresses to hosts on a network. You learned how to configure Linux servers to use DHCP to obtain their networking information and how to assign static IP addresses.

You learned that the **ifup** and **ifdown** scripts are available on many linux distributions and that they can be used to easily bring up or down a network interface. Finally, you learned about GUI and TUI tools that you can use to configure the networking settings on a Linux server.

Quiz

1. What command can be used to display the hostname of a Linux system?

   a. hostname

   b. uname -n

   c. hostname -f

   d. All of the above.

2. Entries added to the /etc/hosts file become automatically available in DNS.

   a. True

   b. False

3. Which configuration file controls the order in which lookups are performed?

   a. /var/nsswitch.conf

   b. /etc/nsswitch.conf

   c. /etc/resolv.conf

   d. /var/resolv.conf

4. What range of ports are considered unprivileged ports?

   a. 0 - 1023

   b. 0 - 1000

   c. 1024 - 2048

d. 1024 - 65535

5. DHCP stands for Dynamic Host Configuration Protocol.

a. True

b. False

Quiz Answers

1. D

2. B

3. B

4. D

5. A

Network Troubleshooting

Network troubleshooting is a large and complex topic. How you approach a situation will largely depend on the circumstances and environment in which you are doing the network troubleshooting. However, in this chapter, you will learn some of the most common tools you can use to perform network diagnostics.

First you'll learn about the ping command and how to test network connectivity with it. Next you'll learn how to examine network routes using the traceroute and tracepath commands. You'll also learn how to see various network statistics with the netstat command. We'll cover how to analyze raw network traffic using tcpdump. Finally, you'll learn how to test if a port is actually open by connecting to it with the telnet command.

Ping

If you are having trouble connecting to a host over a network, one of the first things you can is to ping the host. The **ping** command sends one or more ICMP packets to a host that you specify and waits for a reply.

To use the ping command, simply run **ping** and provide a hostname or IP address. By default, **ping** will keep sending packets until you stop the program with **Control-C**. If you want to specify the number of packets to send, use the **-c** option. For example, to send three packets to google.com run **ping -c 3 google.com**.

Here is the output of a ping command.

```
$ ping -c 3 google.com
PING google.com (2.5.2.7) 56 bytes of data.
64 bytes from 2.5.2.7: icmp_seq=1 ttl=53 time=20.1 ms
64 bytes from 2.5.2.7: icmp_seq=2 ttl=53 time=20.2 ms
64 bytes from 2.5.2.7: icmp_seq=3 ttl=53 time=23.9 ms

--- google.com ping statistics ---
3 packets transmitted, 3 received, 0% packet loss,
time 2004ms
rtt min/avg/max/mdev = 21.489/22.924/24.154/1.111 ms
```

You should notice that the hostname was translated into an IP address. In this case, google.com resolved to 2.5.2.7. If the name doesn't resolve you'll get an "unknown host" error. In that case you should use the IP, address of the system you are trying to connect to. Also, if you can ping by IP address but not by name, there is a problem with the resolution of the DNS name.

That ping command sent three packets. The statistics section reported that 3 replies were received and thus no packet loss was encountered. This means we have network connectivity to google.com. You'll also notice that each packet has a time associated with it. In this example the first reply was received in 20 milliseconds as was the second packet. The third reply took 23.9 milliseconds. You'll see a summary of this activity on the last line in the output. RTT stands for "Round Trip Time".

Here is an example where no replies were received. You'll see that

100% packet loss is reported. This means there is no network connectivity between this host and google.com.

```
$ ping -c 3 google.com
PING google.com (2.5.2.7) 56 bytes of data.
From 2.5.2.7 icmp_seq=1 Destination Host Unreachable
From 2.5.2.7 icmp_seq=2 Destination Host Unreachable
From 2.5.2.7 icmp_seq=3 Destination Host Unreachable

--- google.com ping statistics ---
3 packets transmitted, 0 received, +3 errors, 100%
packet loss, time 2002ms
pipe 3
```

Here is an example where no replies were received. You'll see that 100% packet loss is reported. This means there is no network connectivity between this host and google.com.

At this point, the only thing we know is we can't ping google.com. It doesn't necessarily mean that google.com is down. At this point, I should try to ping something on my local network. If I cannot ping anything on my local network, then I have a problem with my host. Maybe my network cable was accidentally disconnected. Maybe I performed an upgrade on my server and the network drivers didn't update properly. Maybe I forget to start the networking services on my server after I performed some maintenance. The point is I at least know where to start looking.

If I could successfully ping another host on my local network, then the problem lies outside of my system. Maybe the router on the edge of my company's network is down and I cannot reach any hosts on the public internet. We could test that scenario by pinging other hosts like facebook.com or youtube.com. If we can ping Facebook and Youtube, then it's a problem specifically getting to Google. Perhaps Google installed a firewall that simply discards ICMP packets and thus pings will never work. If that turns out to be the case, then we'll need to use other tools to test network connectivity, which we'll be covering soon.

This example demonstrates pinging an IP address. This IP address is on same local network as the host I'm running the command from and the responce times are very fast. It's less than 1 millisecond in fact.

```
$ ping -c 3 10.0.2.2
PING 10.0.2.2 (10.0.2.2) 56(84) bytes of data.
64 bytes from 10.0.2.2: icmp_seq=1 ttl=63 time=0.272
ms
64 bytes from 10.0.2.2: icmp_seq=2 ttl=63 time=0.103
ms
64 bytes from 10.0.2.2: icmp_seq=3 ttl=63 time=0.202
ms

--- 10.0.2.2 ping statistics ---
3 packets transmitted, 3 received, 0% packet loss,
time 2001ms
rtt min/avg/max/mdev = 0.103/0.192/0.272/0.070 ms
```

Trace Route

Ping tests an endpoint, but it doesn't tell you anything about the path or route the network packets take. To examine the route, use the **traceroute** command. Note that the **traceroute** command requires root privileges to function properly.

By default, **traceroute** will attempt to translate IP addresses into DNS names. If you want to skip that step and just work with IP address, use the **-n** option. This will speed things up a bit and can be helpful if you are experiencing DNS issues. This output is easier to read than DNS names, in my opinion.

```
# traceroute -n google.com
traceroute to google.com (2.5.2.7), 30 hops max, 60
byte packets
Diagnosing Network Connections 413
 1  10.0.2.2  0.296 ms  0.178 ms  0.220 ms
 2  192.168.1.1  2.529 ms  2.713 ms  2.630 ms
 3  72.14.237.231  23.750 ms  22.087 ms 12.12.132.137
22.701 ms
 4  216.58.216.78  20.549 ms 12.250.16.30  22.904 ms
```

```
216.58.216.78   20.724 ms
```

The **traceroute** command sends 3 packets to each hop along the way. You can see the response times for each hop along the route. The first hop is very quick while the last hop is slower. This is expected behavior. However, if one of the hops along the path takes a very long time to respond, that's an indication of where an issue may exist. Maybe there is network congestion on that particular router, for instance.

If you see an asterisk where you normally see times, that means a reply wasn't received. Some routers are actually configured to block **traceroute** data. In these cases the **traceroute** command may be of little use to you. If network connectivity is otherwise working and you see asterisks in the **traceroute** output, that probably means a router is blocking **traceroute** data and not that there is an actual problem.

Network troubleshooting consists of looking at the same situation from multiple angles, using multiple tools, and drawing conclusions from the overall picture. It also helps to know how your particular network is configured. Situational awareness is the key to network troubleshooting. You cannot simply rely on one tool like **ping** or **traceroute** and be guaranteed you know what is happening on a network.

An alternative to **traceroute** is **tracepath**. The tracepath command does not require root privileges. You can use the **-n** option to use IP addresses instead of DNS names just like you can with **traceroute**.

The **tracepath** command will produce one line of output for each response it receives, unlike **tracreoute** which produces one line of output per hop. In the following example, you'll see that two responses were received from 10.0.2.2.

```
$ tracepath -n google.com
 1?: [LOCALHOST]     pmtu 1500
 1:   10.0.2.2        0.470ms
 1:   10.0.2.2        0.649ms
```

```
2:   192.168.1.1    2.147ms asymm 64
...
```

For simple checks, **tracepath** can do the trick. For advanced options, you'll probably end up using **traceroute**.

Network Statistics

The **netstat** command can be used to collect a wide variety of network information. Here are some of my favorite and most used netstat options.

-n   Display numerical addresses and ports.

-i   Displays a list of network interfaces.

-r   Displays the route table. (**netstat -rn**)

-p   Display the PID and program used.

-l   Display listening sockets. (**netstat -nlp**)

-t   Limit the output to TCP (**netstat -ntlp**)

-u   Limit the output to UDP (**netstat -nulp**)

The **-n** option is used to display numerical IP addresses and ports as opposed to hostnames and service names. You can use this option in conjunction with most other netstat options.

Get a list of network interfaces on your system by using the **-i** option.

To display routing information, use **-r**. I often use **netstat -rn** to display the routes using IP addresses.

The **-p** option displays the PID and program that is using a given socket. For example, if you are connected via SSH to a server and you run **netstat -p**, you will see the PID of the specific SSH process you are connected to. Note that you'll need to use root privileges with the **-p** option.

The **-l** option displays listening sockets. Use this option in conjunction with the **-p** option to see what processes are listening on what ports. On a web server, for example, it will show that a process such as **nginx** or **apache** is listening on port 80. If you cannot connect to a given port on a system, run this command to make sure that a process is actually listening on that port.

You can limit the output of **netstat** to a specific protocol. To limit output to the TCP protocol, use **netstat -t**. For UDP, use the **-u** option. If you want a list of all programs that are listening on tcp ports, you can use **netstat -ntlp**.

Here is some sample output from the **netstat** command. The first bit of output is a list of network interfaces from the **netstat -i** command. Next, the routing information is displayed with **netstat -rn**. Finally, a list of programs that are listening on TCP ports is displayed. In this example, SSH is listening on port 22, and a program called **master**, which is the Postfix master process, is listening on the SMTP port, port 25. Remember to use root privileges with the **-p** option. I accomplished that by using the **sudo** command.

```
[jason@linuxsvr ~]$ netstat -i
Kernel Interface table
Iface    MTU  RX-OK RX-ERR RX-DRP RX-OVR   TX-OK TX-
ERR TX-DRP TX-OVR Flg
eth0    1500   3975      0      0 0         2627
0       0      0 BMRU
lo     65536      8      0      0 0            8
0       0      0 LRU
[jason@linuxsvr ~]$ netstat -rn
Kernel IP routing table
Destination Gateway     Genmask          Flags   MSS
Window  irtt Iface
0.0.0.0     10.0.2.2    0.0.0.0          UG         0 0
0 eth0
```

```
10.0.2.0    0.0.0.0      255.255.255.0    U         0 0
0 eth0
[jason@linuxsvr ~]$ sudo netstat -ntlp
Active Internet connections (only servers)
Proto Recv-Q Send-Q Local Address  Foreign Address
State    PID/Program name
tcp        0       0 0.0.0.0:22      0.0.0.0:*
LISTEN   943/sshd
tcp        0       0 127.0.0.1:25    0.0.0.0:*
LISTEN   1313/master
```

Packet Sniffing

Sometimes it's not enough to know that network connectivity is in place. Sometimes you need to examine the contents of the network traffic to ensure payloads are actually being delivered. Perhaps one host is claiming to send data to another; to be sure that data is reaching its destination, you can look at the traffic it is receiving. To do this, you'll want to use some sort of packet sniffing tool, such as **tcpdump**.

Even though there are several other tools that perform this same task, **tcpdump** is one of the older and most commonly installed tools. It requires root privileges to run. If you run it without arguments, it prints out a description of the contents of network packets being received.

It will display information such as a timestamp, the source system address and port, the destination system address and port, and packet specific information. The **tcpdump** utility will continue to examine packets until you stop it with **Control-c**.

Like other networking commands we've covered, **tcpdump** uses the **-n** option to both suppress DNS queries and display numerical addresses and ports.

To display information in ASCII—or human readable—format, use the **-A** option. This will allow you to see human readable text, if that type of data is being received on the host. For example, if you are using

tcpdump to examine incoming traffic on a webserver, you can see the URL paths that are being requested if you use the **-A** option.

If you want even more output and information, use the **-v** option. To increase the verbosity, use **-vv**; for the most verbosity, use **-vvv**.

The following is some sample output from **tcpdump**. On the far left hand side of the output is the time stamp. Next is the source information followed by the destination. Finally, information about the network packet is displayed at the end of the line.

```
$ sudo tcpdump
tcpdump: verbose output suppressed, use -v or -vv for
full protocol decode
listening on eth0, link-type EN10MB (Ethernet),
capture size 65535 bytes
19:25:49.639495 IP linuxsvr.ssh > 10.0.2.2.64440:
Flags [P.], seq 3312803324:3312803408, ack 2443835,
win 40880, length 84
19:25:49.639586 IP linuxsvr.ssh > 10.0.2.2.64440:
Flags [P.], seq 84:120, ack 1, win 40880, length 36
19:25:49.639750 IP 10.0.2.2.64440 > linuxsvr.ssh:
Flags [.], ack 84, win 65535, length 0
19:25:49.639763 IP 10.0.2.2.64440 > linuxsvr.ssh:
Flags [.], ack 120, win 65535, length 0
```

The following output shows an example of verbose ASCII output. You'll notice that a client requested the **/about** page from the web server on this host. Remember to use root privileges when executing tcpdump.

```
 $ sudo tcpdump -Anvvv
tcpdump: listening on eth0, link-type EN10MB
(Ethernet), capture size 65535 bytes
19:44:27.067530 IP (tos 0x10, ttl 64, id 5120, offset
0, flags [DF], proto TCP (6), length 64)
    10.0.2.44.37534 > 10.0.2.15.80: Flags [P.], cksum
0xfe34 (incorrect -> 0xce40), seq 1:13, ack 1, win
683, options [nop,nop,TS val 1585227 ecr 1584441],
length 12
E..@..@.@.(............P..>.:........OK..-9GET /about
```

Telnet

The **telnet** command is practically obsolete. It was originally used to log into remote systems. Today, SSH has taken its place, but **telnet** can be used in network troubleshooting. Since **telnet** has fallen out of favor for interactive logins, it may not be installed by default on some linux distributions.

You can use **telnet** to initiate a TCP connection to a host on a specific port. Let's go back to a previous hypothetical situation. Let's say we cannot ping google.com from our host. We know that in and of itself doesn't necessarily mean that google.com is down. To see if google.com is accepting web traffic, we can connect to the HTTP port, which is port 80. To do this, we type **telnet google.com 80**.

If the port is open, we'll get a message like "connected to google.com." If you want to, you can send data directly to the port by typing in some data. The HTTP protocol does accept human readable commands. For example, to request a web page, use "GET" followed by the path. To get the home page, type "GET /". Once you are ready to close the connection, hold down the ctrl key and press the right bracket key (**^]**). This will bring you to a telnet prompt. To exit telnet, type **quit** and press enter.

When you connect, you may get a message like "operation timed out" or "connection refused". "Operation timed out" means a connection could not be established. This could because traffic is silently getting dropped before it reaches the port or that port is not open on that host. If you get a "connection refused" message, that means the port is being blocked by a firewall.

```
$ telnet google.com 80
Trying 216.58.2.7...
Connected to google.com.
Escape character is '^]'.
GET /
HTTP/1.0 200 OK
```

```
^]
telnet> quit
closed.
```

Summary

In this chapter, you learned how the **ping** command can be used to determine if network connectivity exists between two hosts. You also learned that even if **ping** fails it does not necessarily mean the host you are pinging is down.

Next you learned how to trace the path network traffic takes on the way to a host. You also learned how to list network interfaces, show the route table, and display the applications that are listening on ports by using the **netstat** command.

We also covered how to perform sniff network packets using **tcpdump**. Finally, you learned how to test for port connectivity with the **telnet** command.

Quiz

1. Which commands can be used for network troubleshooting?

   a. ping

   b. traceroute

   c. netstat

   d. tcpdump

   e. All of the above.

2. If you can't ping a host, you can always be assured that the host you are attempting to ping is down.

   a. True

   b. False

3. If you can ping by IP address but not by name, there is a problem with the resolution of the DNS name.

   a. True

   b. False

Quiz Answers

1. E

2. B

3. A

Process Management

Listing Processes and Displaying Information

To display the currently running processes, use the **ps** command. If no options are specified, **ps** will display the processes associated with your current session. To see every process, including ones that are not owned by you, use **ps -e**. To see processes running by a specific user, use **ps -u username**.

ps - Display process status.

Common **ps** options:

-e - Everything, all processes.

-f - Full format listing.

-u username - Display processes running as username.

-p pid - Display process information for pid. A PID is a process ID.

Common **ps** commands:

ps -e - Display all processes.

ps -ef - Display all processes with a full format listing.

ps -eH - Display a process tree.

ps -e --forest - Display a process tree.

ps -u username - Display processes running as username.

```
$ ps
  PID TTY          TIME CMD
19511 pts/2     00:00:00 bash
19554 pts/2     00:00:00 ps
$ ps -p 19511
  PID TTY          TIME CMD
19511 pts/2     00:00:00 bash
$ ps -f
UID          PID  PPID  C STIME TTY          TIME CMD
bob        19511 19509  0 16:50 pts/2    00:00:00 -bash
bob        19556 19511  0 16:50 pts/2    00:00:00 ps -f
$ ps -e | head
  PID TTY          TIME CMD
    1 ?        00:00:02 init
    2 ?        00:00:00 kthreadd
    3 ?        00:00:19 ksoftirqd/0
    5 ?        00:00:00 kworker/0:0H
    7 ?        00:00:00 migration/0
    8 ?        00:00:00 rcu_bh
    9 ?        00:00:17 rcu_sched
   10 ?        00:00:12 watchdog/0
   11 ?        00:00:00 khelper
$ ps -ef | head
UID          PID  PPID  C STIME TTY          TIME CMD
root           1     0  0 Dec27 ?        00:00:02 /sbin/init
root           2     0  0 Dec27 ?        00:00:00 [kthreadd]
root           3     2  0 Dec27 ?        00:00:19 [ksoftirqd/0]
root           5     2  0 Dec27 ?        00:00:00 [kworker/0:0H]
root           7     2  0 Dec27 ?        00:00:00 [migration/0]
root           8     2  0 Dec27 ?        00:00:00 [rcu_bh]
root           9     2  0 Dec27 ?        00:00:17 [rcu_sched]
```

```
root            10      2   0 Dec27 ?     00:00:12 [watchdog/0]
root            11      2   0 Dec27 ?     00:00:00 [khelper]
$ ps -fu www-data
UID           PID  PPID  C STIME TTY        TIME CMD
www-data      941   938  0 Dec27 ?     00:00:00
/usr/sbin/apache2 -k start
www-data      942   938  0 Dec27 ?     00:00:00
/usr/sbin/apache2 -k start
www-data      943   938  0 Dec27 ?     00:00:00
/usr/sbin/apache2 -k start
```

Here are other commands that allow you to view running processes.

pstree - Display running processes in a tree format.

top - Interactive process viewer.

htop - Interactive process viewer. This command is less common than **top** and may not be available on the system.

Running Processes in the Foreground and Background

Up until this point, all the commands you have executed have been running in the foreground. When a command, process, or program is running in the foreground, the shell prompt will not be displayed until that process exits. For long running programs, it can be convenient to send them to the background. Processes that are backgrounded still execute and perform their task; however, they do not block you from entering further commands at the shell prompt. To background a process, place an ampersand (&) at the end of the command.

command & - Start command in the background.

Ctrl-c - Kill the foreground process.

Ctrl-z - Suspend the foreground process.

bg [%num] - Background a suspended process.

fg [%num] - Foreground a background process.

kill [%num] - Kill a process by job number or PID.

jobs [%num] - List jobs.

```
$ ./long-running-program &
[1] 22686
$ ps -p 22686
  PID TTY             TIME CMD
22686 pts/1    00:00:00 long-running-pr
$ jobs
[1]+  Running   ./long-running-program &
$ fg
./long-running-program
```

When a command is backgrounded, two numbers are displayed. The number in brackets is the job number and can be referred by preceding it with the percent sign. The second number is the PID. Here is what starting multiple processes in the background looks like.

```
$ ./long-running-program &
[1] 22703
$ ./long-running-program &
[2] 22705
$ ./long-running-program &
[3] 22707
$ ./long-running-program &
[4] 22709


$ jobs
[1]   Done          ./long-running-program
[2]   Done          ./long-running-program
[3]-  Running       ./long-running-program &
[4]+  Running       ./long-running-program &
```

The plus sign (+) in the **jobs** output represents the current job while the minus sign (–) represents the previous job. The current job is considered to be the last job that was stopped while it was in the foreground or the last job started in the background. The current job can be referred to by %% or %+. If no job information is supplied to the fg or bg commands, the current job is operated upon. The previous job can be referred to by %-.

You will notice that jobs 1 and 2 are reported as being done. The shell does not interrupt your current command line, but will report job statuses right before a new prompt is displayed. For example, if you start a program in the background, a prompt is returned. The shell will not report the status of the job until a new prompt is displayed. You can request a new prompt be displayed simply by hitting **Enter**.

To bring a job back to the foreground, type in the name of the job or use the **fg** command. To foreground the current job, execute %%, %+, **fg**, **fg %%**, **fg %+**, or **fg %num**. To foreground job 3, execute %3 or **fg %3**.

```
$ jobs
[3]-  Running      ./long-running-program &
[4]+  Running      ./long-running-program &
$ fg %3
./long-running-program
```

To pause or suspend a job that is running in the foreground, type **Ctrl-z**. Once a job is suspended it can be resumed in the foreground or background. To background a suspended job, type the name of the job followed by an ampersand or use bg followed by the job name.

```
$ jobs
[1]   Running    ./long-running-program &
[2]-  Running    ./long-running-program &
[3]+  Running    ./another-program &
$ fg
./another-program
^Z
[3]+  Stopped    ./another-program
$ jobs
[1]   Running    ./long-running-program &
[2]-  Running    ./long-running-program &
```

```
[3]+  Stopped    ./another-program
$ bg %3
[3]+ ./another-program &
$ jobs
[1]    Running    ./long-running-program &
[2]-   Running    ./long-running-program &
[3]+   Running    ./another-program &
```

You can stop or kill a background job using the **kill** command. For example, to kill job number 1, execute **kill %1**. To kill a job that is running in the foreground, type **Ctrl-c**.

```
$ jobs
[1]    Running    ./long-running-program &
[2]-   Running    ./long-running-program &
[3]+   Running    ./another-program &
$ kill %1
[1]    Terminated ./long-running-program
$ jobs
[2]-   Running    ./long-running-program &
[3]+   Running    ./another-program &
$ fg %2
./long-running-program
^C
$ jobs
[3]+   Running    ./another-program &
$
```

Killing Processes

Ctrl-c - Kills the foreground process.

kill [signal] pid - Send a signal to a process.

kill -l - Display a list of signals.

The default signal used by kill is termination. You will see this signal referred to as SIGTERM or TERM for short. Signals have numbers that correspond to their names. The default TERM signal is number 15, so running **kill pid, kill -15 pid,** and **kill -TERM pid** are all equivalent. If a process does not terminate when you send it the TERM signal, use the KILL signal, which is number 9.

```
$ ps | grep hard-to-stop
27398 pts/1     00:00:00 hard-to-stop
$ kill 27398
$ ps | grep hard-to-stop
27398 pts/1     00:00:00 hard-to-stop
$ kill -9 27398
$ ps | grep hard-to-stop
$
```

Instead of running the **ps** command and piping its output to the **grep** command, you can use the **pgrep** command, which is built for just this purpose. It prints the PIDs of commands that match the search pattern you supply to it.

pgrep [options] search_pattern

Let's use **pgrep** to determine the PID of the **crond** process.

```
$ pgrep crond
13813
$ ps -fp 13813
UID          PID  PPID  C STIME TTY          TIME CMD
root        13813    1  0 20:47 ?        00:00:00
/usr/sbin/crond -n
```

If multiple matches exist, the PIDs of each of the matches is returned. In this example, we are searching for "nd", which happens to match **crond** and **systemd-logind**.

```
$ pgrep nd
13813
13949
$ ps -fp 13813 13949
UID          PID  PPID  C STIME TTY      STAT    TIME
CMD
```

```
root      13813     1  0 20:47 ?        Ss      0:00
/usr/sbin/crond -n
root      13949     1  0 20:47 ?        Ss      0:00
/usr/lib/systemd/systemd-logind
```

If you want to perform an exact match, use the **-x** option. This example demonstrates that "nd" does not match any process exactly, so no PIDs are returned. However, searching for "crond" does exactly match one process.

```
$ pgrep -x nd
$ pgrep -x crond
13813
$ ps -fp 13813
UID         PID  PPID  C STIME TTY          TIME CMD
root      13813     1  0 20:47 ?       00:00:00
/usr/sbin/crond -n
```

The **pkill** command acts in much the same was the **pgrep** command, except it sends the TERM signal to the matching processes by default. You can send a different signal in the same manner as the **kill** command. This example kills the **crond** process. We use the **pgrep** command to ensure the process is indeed killed.

```
# pkill crond
# pgrep crond
#
```

You can also kill a process by name with the **killall** command. The **killall** command is similar to the **kill** and **pkill** commands.

killall [options] process_name

For example, to kill all the **httpd** process, run this command.

```
# killall httpd
```

If the **httpd** processes didn't die, you can use the KILL signal as we did in a previous example.

```
# killall -9 httpd
```

You can also use the **killall** command to kill all the processes for a given user by using the **-u** option followed by the username. A normal user cannot kill another user's processes. The only exception is for the superuser, the root account. Root can kill anyone's processes on a system. This is an example of using the root account to kill all of the processes that are being executed by the user john.

```
# killall -u john
```

To show when a process gets killed by the **kill** command, use the **-v** option.

```
# killall -vu john
Killed bash(624) with signal 15
```

Process Priorities and Niceness

All processes on a Linux system are assigned a niceness value. The niceness value ranges from -20 to 19, with -20 being the highest priorty and 19 being the lowest priority. Processes with higher priority get scheduled to run more often. You can think of processes with higher niceness numeric values as being nice to the processes that have lower niceness numeric values. For example, a process with a niceness of 10 will be "nice" to a process with a priorty of 0 and allow it to run at a higher priority. The process with the niceness of 0 will get more CPU time than the process with the niceness of 10.

To view the niceness value of a given process, use the **-l** option of the **ps** command. The niceness value is listed in the **NI** column. In this example, the niceness value is 0 for both processes shown.

```
$ ps -l
F S   UID   PID  PPID  C PRI  NI ADDR SZ WCHAN   TTY
TIME CMD
0 S  1000  1972  1971  0  80   0 - 28838 wait    pts/0
00:00:00 bash
0 R  1000 22893  1972  0  80   0 - 30319 -       pts/0
00:00:00 ps
```

You can also give **ps** a format to use with the **-o** option followed by a comma separated list of columns you would like to display.   This command displays the PID, the niceness, and the command.

```
$ ps -o pid,nice,cmd
  PID  NI CMD
 1972   0 -bash
22922   0 ps -o pid,nice,cmd
```

Additionally, you can also use the **top** command to view the niceness of processes. Like the **ps** command, the niceness value is listed in the **NI** column.

```
top - 22:25:27 up  2:55,  1 user,  load average: 0.00, 0.01, 0.05
Tasks:  82 total,   2 running,  80 sleeping,   0 stopped,   0 zombie
%Cpu(s):  0.0 us,   0.0 sy,   0.0 ni,100.0 id,   0.0 wa,   0.0 hi,   0.0 si,   0.0
st
KiB Mem :  1018256 total,    272180 free,    114936 used,    631140 buff/cache
KiB Swap:  2047996 total,   2047988 free,         8 used.    721392 avail Mem

PID USER      PR  NI    VIRT    RES    SHR S %CPU %MEM     TIME+ COMMAND
  1 root      20   0   54180   3900   2412 S  0.0  0.4   0:00.90 systemd
  2 root      20   0       0      0      0 S  0.0  0.0   0:00.00 kthreadd
  3 root      20   0       0      0      0 S  0.0  0.0   0:00.30 ksoftirqd/0
  5 root       0 -20       0      0      0 S  0.0  0.0   0:00.00 kworker/0:0H
  6 root      20   0       0      0      0 S  0.0  0.0   0:00.11 kworker/u2:0
  7 root      rt   0       0      0      0 S  0.0  0.0   0:00.00 migration/0
```

To view the default niceness value, use the **nice** command without any arguments. Typcially, the default niceness value for normal users is 0.

```
$ nice
0
$
```

To start a process, or program, with a different niceness level, run **nice -n ADJUSTMENT COMMAND**. Let's assume you want to convert a very large video file from one format to another. This type of process will be very CPU intensive. You don't want this process to make your Linux system unresponsive because you are currently using it for other, more important tasks. Additionally, you are not concerned with the amount of time it takes to convert the video. You can start this process at a lower priority by running the following command.

```
$ nice -n 10 avconv -i movie.avi movie.mp4
```

Since the default nicencess value is 0 and an offset of 10 was applied, the niceness value of the process will be 10. Let's check the niceness of this process with the **ps** command.

```
$ ps -o pid,nice,cmd
1394    0 /bin/bash
 3815   10 avconv -I movie.avi movie.mp4
```

What if you want to change the niceness of a process that is already running? Use the **renice** command, supplying the new niceness value after **-n** and end the command with the PID of the process you are altering. Let's change the niceness value to the lowest priorty with this command.

```
$ renice -n 19 3815
3815 (process ID) old priority 10, new priority 19
```

If you attempt to lower the niceness value, you will get a permission denied error. This is because only the superuser can set the niceness value to a lower number, giving a process a higher priority than it currently has. Said another way, normal users can only make their processes nicer.

```
$ renice -n 0 3815
renice: failed to set priority for 3815 (process ID):
Permission denied
$ su -
Password:
# renice -n 0 3815
3815 (process ID) old priority 19, new priority 0
```

Processes and Disconnecting from Your Session

When you log out of a Linux system, all of your processes associated with that session are sent the **SIGHUP**, or hangup, signal. This effectively kills all of the processes associated with your session. If you want to leave a process running after you log out, you can use the **nohup** command. The **nohup** command will ignore the **SIGHUP** signal, allowing the process to continue running.

`nohup COMMAND [command_arguments]`

The output generated by the command supplied to **nohup** will be saved in a file called **nohup.out**, located in the directory in which you started the process. To save the output to a different file, use redirection.

Typically, the **nohup** command is used to background a process. This example starts a shell script called **do-backup.sh** in the background with the **nohup** command. If you log out and log back in again, you can see that the process is still running and the output is being sent to the **nohup.out** file.

```
$ nohup do-backup.sh &
[1] 23364
nohup: ignoring input and appending output to
'nohup.out'
$ exit
Connection to linuxsvr closed
$ ssh linuxsvr
$ ps -fp 23364
UI        PID  PPID  C STIME TTY  TIME CMD
jason   23364     1  0 18:31 ?    00:00:00 do-backup.sh
$ cat nohup.out
Apr  5 18:34:20 - Creating backup.
$
```

If we wanted to redirect the output to a file other than **nohup.out**, we would use the greater-than sign followed by a file.

```
$ nohup do-backup.sh > /var/tmp/backup.log &
[1] 23401
nohup: ignoring input and redirecting stderr to
stdout
$ cat /var/tmp/backup.log
Apr  5 18:37:24 - Creating backup.
$
```

You can also use a terminal multiplexer to accomplish the same task. The two most popular terminal multiplexers are GNU Screen and tmux. To leave processes running in the background, first start the terminal multiplexer program. Next, start the process you would like to keep running after you log out. Finally, detach from your terminal multiplexer. When you log out, the terminal multiplexer and all of its child processes are still running. You can then come back at a later time and reattach to the session.

Here is an example using GNU Screen. To start Screen, run the **screen** command. It may not appear as if anything has happened, but you are now in a screen session. To list the sessions, use the **-ls** option. Now you can start the process you want to ensure stays running after you have disconnected. We won't bother starting it in the background since **screen** will be caputuring the output. To disconnect from the screen session, type **Ctrl-A** followed by **D**. If you run **screen -ls** again, it will show that a screen session is running, but you are not attached to it. At this point, you can disconnect from the server and Screen, as well as any processes started with it, will continue to run. To reconnect to a screen session, use the **-r** option. If there are multiple screen sessions, you will need to supply the session name as it is displayed in the **screen -ls** output.

```
[jason@laptop ~]$ ssh linuxsvr
[jason@linuxsvr ~]$ screen
[jason@linuxsvr ~]$ screen -ls
There is a screen on: 23478.pts-0.linuxsvr (Attached)
1 Socket in /var/run/screen/S-jason.
[jason@linuxsvr ~]$ do-backup.sh
Apr  5 18:42:51 - Creating backup
[detached from 23478.pts-0.linuxsvr]
[jason@linuxsvr ~]$ screen -ls
There is a screen on: 23478.pts-0.linuxsvr (Detached)
1 Socket in /var/run/screen/S-jason.
[jason@linuxsvr ~]$ exit
Connection to linuxsvr closed.
[jason@laptop ~]$ ssh linuxsvr
[jason@linuxsvr ~]$ screen -r
Apr  5 18:53:51 - Backup complete
[jason@linuxsvr ~]$
```

Load Average

You may have noticed the words **load average** followed by a series of three numbers in the output of the **top** command. The first number is the load average over the last minute, the second number is the load average over the last five minutes, and the final number is the load average over the last 15 minutes. Here is some example output from the **top** command.

```
top - 20:41:23 up  5:07,  2 users,  load average:
0.90, 2.32, 1.05
```

The load average represents how busy a system is. A system with a load average of 0.00 is completely idle. In general, you can think of load average as the number of processes using or waiting for CPU time. The actual calculation is a bit more complex and includes processes that are waiting on other resources including I/O operations such as reading from or writing to a disk. However, a load average without context is meaningless. You need to know how many CPUs a system has in order to determine what a given load average means.

Let's say a single CPU Linux system has the following load average: 0.80, 1.75, and 5.00. This means that over that last minute the CPU was utilized 80% of the time. You could also say that the CPU was idle 20% of the time. Over the last five minutes, the CPU was overloaded by 75% on average. A load average of 1.75 on a single CPU system means that .75 processes had to wait for a turn to run on that CPU. Over the last 15 minutes, the load was 5.00, meaning that the system was overloaded by 400%.

If we take the same load averages of 0.80, 1.75, and 5.00 on a system that has 16 CPUs, then the meaning of those numbers change dramatically. Having a load average of 5.00 on a single CPU system is a very high load average, while having that same load average on a 16 CPU system means that only about 31% of the system resources are in use.

To view the number of CPUs in your system, look at the **/proc/cpuinfo** fie. Here is a single CPU system.

```
$ cat /proc/cpuinfo
processor       : 0
vendor_id       : GenuineIntel
cpu family      : 6
model           : 61
model name      : Intel(R) Core(TM) i7-5557U CPU @
3.10GHz
stepping        : 4
microcode       : 0x19
cpu MHz         : 3103.175
cache size      : 6144 KB
physical id     : 0
siblings        : 1
core id         : 0
cpu cores       : 1
apicid          : 0
initial apicid  : 0
fpu             : yes
fpu_exception   : yes
cpuid level     : 5
wp              : yes
flags           : fpu vme de pse tsc msr pae mce cx8
apic sep mtrr pge mca cmov pat pse36 clflush mmx fxsr
sse sse2 syscall nx rdtscp lm constant_tsc rep_good
nopl pni monitor ssse3 lahf_lm
bogomips        : 6206.35
clflush size    : 64
cache_alignment : 64
address sizes   : 39 bits physical, 48 bits virtual
power management:
```

In addition to the **top** command, you can view the load average with the **uptime** and **w** commands.

```
$ uptime
21:11:53 up 5:38, 2 users ,load average: 1.08, 2.03, 4.35
```

```
$ w
21:11:59 up 5:38, 2 users ,load average: 1.08, 2.03, 4.35
USER    TTY    FROM         LOGIN@   IDLE    JCPU    PCPU WHAT
jason   pts/0  10.0.2.2     18:52    4.00s   0.01s   0.01s
screen -r
ellen   pts/1  :pts/0:S.0   18:52    4.00s  47.65s   0.00s w
```

Memory Usage

The **top** command also displays memory utilization for a system.

```
top - 21:16:03 up  5:42,   2 users,   load average: 1.07, 0.60, 0.28
Tasks:  89 total,   3 running,  86 sleeping,   0 stopped,   0 zombie
%Cpu(s): 94.2 us,   5.8 sy, 0.0 ni, 0.0 id,  0.0 wa,  0.0 hi,  0.0 si,   0.0 st
KiB Mem : 1018256 total,    223076 free,   117360 used,    677820 buff/cache
KiB Swap: 2047996 total,  2047988 free,        8 used.   718068 avail Mem
```

You can also use the **free** command to display memory usage. To display in units of megabytes, use the **-m** option. To display in gigabytes, use the **-g** option. Use the **-t** option to display the totals.

```
$ free -m
        total  used  free shared  buff/cache   available
Mem:      994   114   217      6         661         701
Swap:    1999     0  1999
$ free -mt
        total  used  free shared  buff/cache   available
Mem:      994   114   217      6         661         701
Swap:    1999     0  1999
Total:   2994   114  2217
```

Scheduling Repeated Jobs with Cron

If you need to repeat a task on a schedule, you can use the cron service. Every minute, the cron service checks to see if there are any scheduled jobs to run and if so runs them. Cron jobs are often used to automate a process or perform routine maintenance. You can schedule cron jobs by using the `crontab` command.

`cron` - A time based job scheduling service. This service is typically started when the system boots.

crontab - A program to create, read, update, and delete your job schedules.

A crontab (cron table) is a configuration file that specifies when commands are to be executed by cron. Each line in a crontab represents a job and contains two pieces of information: 1) when to run and 2) what to run. The time specification consists of five fields: minute, hour, day of the month, month, and day of the week. After the time specification, you provide the command to be executed.

Crontab Format

```
* * * * * command
| | | | |
| | | | +-- Day of the Week   (0-6)
| | | +---- Month of the Year (1-12)
| | +------ Day of the Month  (1-31)
| +-------- Hour              (0-23)
+---------- Minute            (0-59)
```

The command will only be executed when all of the time specification fields match the current date and time. You can specify that a command be run only once, but this is not the typical use case for cron. Typically, one or more of the time specification fields will contain an asterisk (*) which matches any time or date for that field. Here is an example crontab.

```
# Run every Monday at 07:00.
0 7 * * 1 /opt/sales/bin/weekly-report
```

Here is a graphical representation of the above crontab entry.

```
0 7 * * 1 /opt/sales/bin/weekly-report
| | | | |
| | | | +-- Day of the Week   (0-6)
| | | +---- Month of the Year (1-12)
| | +------ Day of the Month  (1-31)
| +-------- Hour              (0-23)
+---------- Minute            (0-59)
```

This job will run only when the minute is 0, the hour is 7, and the day of the week is 1. In the day of the week, field 0 represents Sunday, 1 Monday, etc. This job will run on any day and during any month since the asterisk was used for those two fields.

If any output is generated by the command, it is mailed to you. You can check your local mail with the **mail** command. If you prefer not to get email, you can redirect the output of the command as in this example.

```
# Run at 02:00 every day and send output to a log.
0 2 * * * /opt/acme/bin/backup > /tmp/backup.log 2>&1
```

You can provide multiple values for each of the fields. If you would like to run a command every half-hour, you could do this.

```
# Run every 30 minutes.
0,30 * * * * /opt/acme/bin/half-hour-check

# Another way to do the same thing.
*/2 * * * * /opt/acme/bin/half-hour-check
```

Instead of using **0,30** for the minute field, you could have used ***/2**. You can even use ranges with a dash. If you want to run a job every minute for the first four minutes of the hour, you can use this time specification: **0-4 * * * * command**.

There are several implementations of the cron scheduler and some allow you to use shortcuts and keywords in your crontabs. Common keywords have been provided below, but refer to the documentation for cron on your system to ensure these will work.

Keyword	Description	Equivalent
@yearly	Run once a year at midnight in the morning on January 1	0 0 1 1 *
@annually	Same as @yearly	0 0 1 1 *
@monthly	Run once a month at midnight in the morning on the first day of the month	0 0 1 * *
@weekly	Run once a week at midnight in the morning on Sunday	0 0 * * 0
@daily	Run once a day at midnight	0 0 * * *
@midnight	Same as @daily	0 0 * * *
@hourly	Run once an hour at the beginning of the hour	0 * * * *
@reboot	Run at startup	N/A

Using the Crontab Command

Use the **crontab** command to manipulate cron jobs.

crontab file - Install a new crontab from file.

crontab -l - List your cron jobs.

crontab -e - Edit your cron jobs.

crontab -r - Remove all of your cron jobs.

```
$ crontab -l
no crontab for bob
$ cat my-cron
# Run every Monday at 07:00.
0 7 * * 1 /opt/sales/bin/weekly-report
$ crontab my-cron
$ crontab -l
# Run every Monday at 07:00.
0 7 * * 1 /opt/sales/bin/weekly-report
$ crontab -e
# $EDITOR is invoked.
$ crontab -r
$ crontab -l
no crontab for bob
$
```

Summary

In this chapter, you learned how to view the running processes with the **ps**, **pstree**, **top**, and **htop** commands. Next, you learned how to start jobs in the background as well as how to view, suspend, resume, and kill those jobs. You also learned how to kill processes with the **kill**, **pkill**, and **killall** commands. Next, process priority and niceness were covered. You learned how to use the **nohup** command to ensure a long running process continues to run even if you disconnect from the Linux system. You also learned about load averages and how to determine the number of CPUs in a Linux system. Finally, you learned how to schedule jobs using the cron service.

Quiz

1. Which command is used to view running processes?

    a. ps

    b. pid

    c. proc

    d. lsproc

2. What character is placed at the end of a command line to start the command in the background?

    a. -

    b. ?

    c. \

    d. &

3. The kill command can be used to kill processes and jobs.

    a. True

    b. False

4. Which command is used to create, read, update, and delete cron jobs?

    a. cron

    b. crond

    c. crontab

    d. vicron

5. Which of the following cron jobs will run at 08:00 AM every day?

    a. 8 0 0 * * /opt/acme/bin/backup

    b. 8 0 * * * /opt/acme/bin/backup

    c. 8 * * * * /opt/acme/bin/backup

    d. 0 8 * * * /opt/acme/bin/backup

Quiz Answers

1. A

2. D

3. A

4. C

5. D

File and Directory Permissions

Looking back at the long listings provided by the **ls** command, you can see that the first bit of information displayed is the permissions for the given file or directory.

```
$ ls -l sales.data
-rw-r--r-- 1 bob users 10400 Sep 27 08:52 sales.data
```

The first character in the permissions string reveals the type. For example, **-** is a regular file, **d** is a directory, and **l** is a symbolic link. Those are the most common types you will encounter. For a full listing, read the **ls** man page.

Symbol	Type
-	Regular file
d	Directory
l	Symbolic link

You will also notice other characters in the permissions string. They represent the three main types of permissions: read, write, and execute. Each one is represented by a single letter, also known as a symbol. Read is represented by **r**, write by **w**, and execute by **x**.

Symbol	Permission
r	Read
w	Write
x	Execute

Read, write, and execute are rather self explanatory. If you have "read" permissions, you can see the contents of the file. If you have "write" permissions, you can modify the file. If you have "execute" permissions, you can run the file as a program. However, when these permissions are applied to directories, they have a slightly different meaning than when they are applied to files.

Permission	File Meaning	Directory Meaning
Read	Allows a file to be read.	Allows file names in the directory to be read.
Write	Allows a file to be modified.	Allows entries to be modified within the directory.
Execute	Allows the execution of a file.	Allows access to contents and metadata for entries in the directory.

There are three categories of users that these permissions can be applied to. These categories—or classes—are user, group, and other. Like the permission types, each set is represented by a single letter. The user who owns the file is represented by **u**, the users in the file's group are represented by **g**, and the other users who do not own the file or are not in the file's group are represented by **o**. The character **a** represents all, meaning user, group, and other. Even though these characters do not show up in an **ls** listing, they can be used to change permissions.

Symbol	Category
u	User
g	Group
o	Other
a	All - user, group, and other.

Every user is a member of at least one group, called their primary group. However, users can and often are members of many groups. Groups are used to organize users into logical sets. For example, if members of the sales team need access to some of the same files and directories, they can be placed into the **sales** group.

Run the **groups** command to see what groups you are a member of. If you supply another users ID as an argument to the **groups** command, you will see the list of groups to which that user belongs. You can also run **id -Gn [user]** to get the same result.

```
$ groups
users sales
$ id -Gn
users sales

$ groups pat
users projectx apache
$ groups jill
users sales manager
```

Secret Decoder Ring for Permissions

Now you have enough background information to start decoding the permissions string. The first character is the type. The next three characters represent the permissions available to the user, also known as the owner of the file. The next three characters represent the permissions available to the members of the file's group. The final three characters represent the permissions available to all others.

In this case, order has meaning. Permission types will be displayed for user, followed by group, and finally for others. Also, the permission types of read, write, and execute are displayed in that order. If a particular permission is not granted, a hyphen (–) will take its place.

Here is a graphical representation of the permission information displayed by **ls -1**.

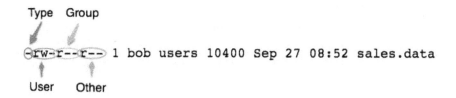

```
-rw-r--r-- 1 bob users 10400 Sep 27 08:52 sales.data
```

If you happen to see an extra character at the end of the permissions string, an alternative access control method has been applied. If you see a period (.), the file or directory has an SELinux (Security Enhanced Linux) security context applied to it. If you see a plus sign (+), ACLs (Access Control Lists) are in use. SELinux and ACLs are beyond the scope of this book. However, you will be pleased to know that the use of either of these is rare. If you are having trouble with permissions and notice an extra character in the permissions string, know that further investigation may be necessary.

```
$ ls -l sales.data.selnx
-rw-r--r--. 1 bob users 1040 Sep 27 08:52 sales.data.selnx
$ ls -l sales.data.acl
-rw-r--r--+ 1 bob users 1040 Sep 27 08:52 sales.data.acl
```

Changing Permissions

Permissions are also known as modes. That is why the command you use to change permissions is called **chmod**, short for "change mode." The format of the chmod command is **chmod mode file**. There are two ways to specify the mode. The first way is called symbolic mode. The symbolic mode format is **chmod user_category operator permission**. Here is a table view of the chmod command symbolic mode format.

Item	Meaning
chmod	The change mode command.
ugoa	The user category. One or more of **u** for user, **g** for group, **o** for other, **a** for all.
+-=	One of **+**, **–**, or **=**. Use **+** to add permissions, **–** to subtract them, or **=** to explicitly set them.
rwx	The permissions. One or more of **r** for read, **w** for write, and **x** for execute.

You can add, subtract, or set permissions using user category and permission pairs. For example, if you want to add the write permission for the members of a file's group, you would specify **chmod g+w file**.

```
$ ls -l sales.data
-rw-r--r-- 1 bob users 10400 Sep 27 08:52 sales.data
$ chmod g+w sales.data
$ ls -l sales.data
-rw-rw-r-- 1 bob users 10400 Sep 27 08:52 sales.data
```

Notice that after running chmod g+w sales.data, the permissions string changed from '-rw-r--r--' to '-rw-rw-r--'. Remember that the permissions are displayed in the order of user, group, and other. The group permission set now includes the **w** symbol, indicating that the write permission has been granted. Now the owner of the file (bob) and members of the group (users) can read and write to the sales.data file. Here is the reverse. This is how you would subtract the write permission.

```
$ ls -l sales.data
-rw-rw-r-- 1 bob users 10400 Sep 27 08:52 sales.data
$ chmod g-w sales.data
$ ls -l sales.data
-rw-r--r-- 1 bob users 10400 Sep 27 08:52 sales.data
```

You can change more than one permission at a time. This time, write and execute permissions are added for the file's group.

```
$ ls -l sales.data
-rw-r--r-- 1 bob users 10400 Sep 27 08:52 sales.data
$ chmod g+wx sales.data
$ ls -l sales.data
-rw-rwxr-- 1 bob users 10400 Sep 27 08:52 sales.data
```

You can even set permissions on different user categories simultaneously. Here is how to change permissions for the user and group. Notice that before running this command, the user already has the write permissions. Using **+** to add permissions does not negate any existing permissions; it just adds to them.

```
$ ls -l sales.data
-rw-r--r-- 1 bob users 10400 Sep 27 08:52 sales.data
$ chmod ug+wx sales.data
$ ls -l sales.data
-rwxrwxr-- 1 bob users 10400 Sep 27 08:52 sales.data
```

If you want to set different permissions for different user categories, you can separate the specifications with a comma. You can mix and match to produce the outcome you desire. Here is how you can specify **rwx** for user while adding **x** for group.

```
$ ls -l sales.data
-rw-r--r-- 1 bob users 10400 Sep 27 08:52 sales.data
$ chmod u=rwx,g+x sales.data
$ ls -l sales.data
-rwxr-xr-- 1 bob users 10400 Sep 27 08:52 sales.data
```

If you want to set the file to be just readable by everyone, run **chmod a=r file**. When you use the equal sign (=), the permissions are set to exactly what you specify. If you specify just read, then only read will be available, regardless of any existing permissions.

```
$ ls -l sales.data
-rw-r--r-- 1 bob users 10400 Sep 27 08:52 sales.data
$ chmod a=r sales.data
$ ls -l sales.data
-r--r--r-- 1 bob users 10400 Sep 27 08:52 sales.data
```

If you do not specify permissions following the equal sign, the permissions are removed. Here is an illustration of this behavior:

```
$ ls -l sales.data
-rw-r--r-- 1 bob users 10400 Sep 27 08:52 sales.data
$ chmod u=rwx,g=rx,o= sales.data
$ ls -l sales.data
-rwxr-x--- 1 bob users 10400 Sep 27 08:52 sales.data
```

Numeric Based Permissions

In addition to symbolic mode, octal mode can be used with **chmod** to set file and directory permissions. Understanding the concepts behind symbolic mode will help you learn octal mode. However, once you learn octal mode, you may find that it is even quicker and easier to use than symbolic mode. Since there are only a few common and practical permission modes, they can be readily memorized and recalled.

In octal mode, permissions are based in binary. Each permission type is treated as a bit that is either set to off (0) or on (1). In permissions, order has meaning. Permissions are always in read, write, and execute order. If **r**, **w**, and **x** are all set to off, the binary representation is 000. If they are all set to on, the binary representation is 111. To represent read and execute permissions while omitting write permissions, the binary number is 101.

r	w	x	
0	0	0	Binary Value for off
1	1	1	Binary Value for on
r	w	w	
0	0	0	Base 10 (decimal) value for off
4	2	1	Base 10 (decimal) value for on

To get a number that can be used with **chmod**, convert the binary representation into base 10 (decimal). The shortcut here is to remember that read equals 4, write equals 2, and execute equals 1. The permissions number is determined by adding up the values for each permission type. There are eight possible values from zero to seven, hence the name octal mode. This table demonstrates all eight of the possible permutations.

Octal	Binary	String	Description
0	000	---	No permissions
1	001	--x	Execute only
2	010	-w-	Write only
3	011	-wx	Write and execute (2 + 1)
4	100	r--	Read only
5	101	r-x	Read and execute (4 + 1)
6	110	rw-	Read and write (4 + 2)
7	111	rwx	Read, write, and execute (4+2+1)

Again, in permissions, order has meaning. The user categories are always ordered as user, group, and other. Once you determine the octal value for each category, you specify them in that order. For example, to get **-rwxr-xr--**, run **chmod 754 file**. That means the user (owner) of the file has read, write, and execute permission; the members of the file's group have read and execute permission; and others have read permissions

```
                U    G    O

Symbolic   rwx  r-x  r--

Binary     111  101  100

Decimal     7    5    4
```

Commonly Used Permissions

Here are the most commonly used permissions. These five permissions will let you do just about anything you need to permissions-wise.

Symbolic	Octal	Use Case / Meaning
`-rwx------`	700	Ensures a file can only be read, edited, and executed by the owner. No others on the system have access.
`-rwxr-xr-x`	755	Allows everyone on the system to execute the file but only the owner can edit it.
`-rw-rw-r--`	664	Allows a group of people to modify the file and let others read it.
`-rw-rw----`	660	Allows a group of people to modify the file and not let others read it.
`-rw-r--r--`	644	Allows everyone on the system to read the file but only the owner can edit it.

When you encounter 777 or 666 permissions, ask yourself "Is there a better way to do this?" "Does everybody on the system need write access to this?" For example, if a script or program is set to 777, then anyone on the system can make changes to that script or program. Since the execute bit is set for everyone, that program can then be executed by anyone on system. If malicious code was inserted either on purpose or on accident, it could cause unnecessary trouble. If multiple people need write access to a file, consider using groups and limiting the access of others. It is good practice to avoid using 777 and 666 permission modes.

Working with Groups

If you work on the sales team and each member needs to update the sales.report file, you would set the group to **sales** using the **chgrp** command and then set the permissions to 664 (**rw-rw-r--**). You could even use 660 (**rw-rw---**) permissions if you want to make sure only members of the sales team can read the report. Technically, 774 (**rwxrwxr--**) or 770 (**rwxrwx---**) permissions work as well, but since sales.report is not an executable program, it makes more sense to use 664 (**rw-rw-r--**) or 660 (**rw-rw----**).

When you create a file, its group is set to your primary group. This behavior can be overridden by using the **newgrp** command, but keep in mind when you create a file it typically inherits your default group. In the following example, Bob's primary group is **users**. Note that the format of the **chgrp** command is **chgrp GROUP FILE**.

```
$ nano sales.report
$ ls -l sales.report
-rw-r--r-- 1 bob users 6 Dec  4 20:41 sales.report
$ chgrp sales sales.report
$ ls -l sales.report
-rw-r--r-- 1 bob sales 6 Dec  4 20:41 sales.report
$ chmod 664 sales.report
$ ls -l sales.report
-rw-rw-r-- 1 bob sales 6 Dec  4 20:41 sales.report
```

Instead of keeping files in the home directories of various team members, it is easier to keep them in a location dedicated to the team. For example, you could ask the system administrator of the server to create a /usr/local/sales directory. The group should be set to **sales** and the permissions should be set to 775 (**rwxrwxr-x**) or 770 (**rwxrwx---**). Use 770 (**rwxrwx---**) if no one outside the sales team needs access to any files, directories, or programs located in /usr/local/sales.

```
$ ls -ld /usr/local/sales
drwxrwxr-x 2 root sales 4096 Dec  4 20:53
/usr/local/sales
$ mv sales.report /usr/local/sales/
$ ls -l /usr/local/sales
total 4
-rw-rw-r-- 1 bob sales 6 Dec  4 20:41 sales.report
```

Directory Permissions Revisited

This example demonstrates how permissions affect directories and their contents. A common problem is having proper permissions set on a file within a directory only to have the incorrect permissions on the directory itself. Not having the correct permissions on a directory can prevent the execution of the file, for example. If you are sure a file's permissions have been set correctly, look at the parent directory. Work your way toward the root of the directory tree by running **ls -ld .** in the current directory, moving up to the parent directory with **cd ..**, and repeating those two steps until you find the problem.

```
$ ls -dl directory/
drwxr-xr-x 2 bob users 4096 Sep 29 22:02 directory/
$ ls -l directory/
total 0
-rwxr--r-- 1 bob users    0 Sep 29 22:02 testprog
$ chmod 400 directory
$ ls -dl directory/
dr-------- 2 bob users 4096 Sep 29 22:02 directory/
$ ls -l directory/
ls: cannot access directory/testprog: Permission
denied
total 0
-????????? ? ? ? ?                ? testprog
$ directory/testprog
-su: directory/testprog: Permission denied
$ chmod 500 directory/
$ ls -dl directory/
dr-x------ 2 bob users 4096 Sep 29 22:02 directory/
```

```
$ ls -l directory/
total 0
-rwxr--r-- 1 bob users 0    Sep 29 22:02 testprog
$ directory/testprog
This program ran successfully.
```

Default Permissions and the File Creation Mask

The file creation mask is what determines the permissions a file will be assigned upon its creation. The mask restricts or masks permissions, thus determining the ultimate permission a file or directory will be given. If no mask were present, directories would be created with 777 (**rwxrwxrwx**) permissions and files would be created with 666 (**rw-rw-rw-**) permissions. The mask can and is typically set by the system administrator, but it can be overridden on a per account basis by including a **umask** statement in your personal initialization files.

umask **[-S]** **[mode]** - Sets the file creation mask to mode if specified. If mode is omitted, the current mode will be displayed. Using the **-S** argument allows umask to display or set the mode with symbolic notation.

The mode supplied to **umask** works in the opposite way as the mode given to **chmod**. When you supply 7 to **chmod**, that is interpreted to mean all permissions on, or **rwx**. When you supply 7 to **umask**, that is interpreted to mean all permissions off, or **---**. Think of **chmod** as turning on, adding, or giving permissions. Think of **umask** as turning off, subtracting, or taking away permissions.

A quick way to estimate what a umask mode will do to the default permissions is to subtract the octal umask mode from 777 in the case of directories and 666 in the case of files. Here is an example of a **umask** **022**, which is typically the default umask used by Linux distributions or set by system administrators.

```
                          Dir      File
Base Permission           777       666
Minus Umask              -022      -022
                         ----      ----
Creation Permission       755       644
```

Using a umask of 002 is ideal for working with members of your group. You will see that when files or directories are created, the permissions allow members of the group to manipulate those files and directories.

```
                          Dir      File
Base Permission           777       666
Minus Umask              -002      -002
                         ----      ----
Creation Permission       775       664
```

Here is another possible umask to use for working with members of your group. Use 007 so that no permissions are granted to users outside of the group.

```
                          Dir      File
Base Permission           777       666
Minus Umask              -007      -007
                         ----      ----
Creation Permission       770       660 *
```

Again, using this octal subtraction method is a good estimation. You can see that the method breaks down with the umask mode of 007. In reality, to get an accurate result each time, you need to convert the octal permissions into binary values. From there, use a bitwise NOT operation on the umask mode and then perform a bitwise AND operation against that and the base permissions.

It is fine to gloss over the subtleties here since there are only a few practical umask modes to use. They are 022, 002, 077, and 007. Save yourself the binary math homework and look at the following table containing all the resulting permissions created by each one of the eight mask permutations.

Octal	Binary	Dir Perms	File Perms
0	000	rwx	rw-
1	001	rw-	rw-
2	010	r-x	r--
3	011	r--	r--
4	100	-wx	-w-
5	101	-w-	-w-
6	110	--x	---
7	111	---	---

Special Modes

Look at this output of umask when the mask is set to 022.

```
$ umask
0022
```

You will notice an extra leading 0. So far, you have only been dealing with three characters that represent permissions for user, group, and other. There is a class of special modes. These modes are **setuid**, **setgid**, and **sticky**. Know that these special modes are declared by prepending a character to the octal mode that you normally use with **umask** or **chmod**. The important point here is to know that **umask 0022** is the same as **umask 022**. Also, **chmod 644** is the same as **chmod 0644**.

Even though special modes will not be covered in this book, they are included here for your reference. There are links at the end of this chapter so you can learn more about these modes if you are so inclined.

setuid permission - Allows a process to run as the owner of the file, not the user executing it.

setgid permission - Allows a process to run with the group of the file, not of the group of the user executing it.

sticky bit - Prevents a user from deleting another user's files even if they would normally have permission to do so.

umask Examples

Here are two examples of the effects umask modes have on file and directory creation.

```
$ umask
0022
$ umask -S
u=rwx,g=rx,o=rx
$ mkdir a-dir
$ touch a-file
$ ls -l
total 4
drwxr-xr-x 2 bob users 4096 Dec  5 00:03 a-dir
-rw-r--r-- 1 bob users    0 Dec  5 00:03 a-file
$ rmdir a-dir
$ rm a-file
$ umask 007
$ umask
0007
$ umask -S
u=rwx,g=rwx,o=
$ mkdir a-dir
$ touch a-file
$ ls -l
total 4
drwxrwx--- 2 bob users 4096 Dec  5 00:04 a-dir
-rw-rw---- 1 bob users    0 Dec  5 00:04 a-file
```

Summary

In this chapter, you learned how to view and manage file and directory permissions. You learned about read, write, and execute permissions and how you can assign those permissions to users, groups, and others. You learned how to use the **chmod** command with symbolic mode as well as octal mode permissions. Next, you learned how to work with groups by using the **newgrp** and **chgrp** commands. Finally, you learned about the file creation mask and how you can control it with the **umask** command.

Resources

- Every Possible Umask Mode - An article that lists every possible umask mode.
  http://linuxtrainingacademy.com/all-umasks

- Linux Permissions Explained Videos
  Watch these two videos that explain and demonstrate Linux file system permissions.
  http://www.linuxtrainingacademy.com/perms/

- Modes - Detailed permission information.
  https://en.wikipedia.org/wiki/Modes_(Unix)

- SELinux - The official SELinux project page.
  http://selinuxproject.org/

- Special File Permissions - An article describing setuid, setgid, and the sticky bit.
  http://docs.oracle.com/cd/E19683-01/806-4078/secfiles-69

- Ubuntu ACL Documentation – This applies not only to Ubuntu, but to other Linux distributions as well.
  http://help.ubuntu.com/community/FilePermissionsACLs

Quiz

1. Given the following output of the **ls -l** command, what permissions are assigned to members of the "staff" group?

   ```
   -rwxrw-r-- 1 jason staff 1040 Sep 27 08:52 sales
   ```

   a. rwx

   b. rw-

   c. r---

   d. −rwxrw-r--

2. Given the following output of the **ls -l** command, what type is "sales"?

   ```
   drwxrw-r-- 1 jason staff 1040 Sep 27 08:52 sales
   ```

   a. file

   b. directory

   c. link

   d. It cannot be determined with the given output.

3. Which command is used to change the permissions on a file or directory?

   a. modch

   b. set

   c. chmod

   d. mkmod

4. The **chmod** command can only be used with numerical permissions.

   a. True

   b. False

5. Every user on a Linux system is in at least one group.

   a. True

   b. False

6. Which command would you run to ensure that "file.txt" can only be read, edited, and executed by the owner and that no other users on the system have access to it?

   a. chmod 777 file.txt

   b. chmod 755 file.txt

   c. chmod 770 file.txt

   d. chmod 700 file.txt

7. Which command is used to set the file creation mask?

   a. fmask

   b. fcmask

   c. umask

   d. chmod

Quiz Answers

1. B

2. B

3. C

4. B

5. A

6. D

7. C

Managing Software

Typically, when you install software on a Linux system you do so with a package. A package is a collection of files that make up an application. Additionally, a package contains data about the application, as well as any steps required to successfully install and remove that application. The data, or metadata, that is contained within a package can include information such as the description of the application, the version of the application, and a list of other packages that it depends on. In order to install or remove a package, you need to use superuser privileges.

A package manager is used to install, upgrade, and remove packages. Any additional software that is required for a package to function properly is known as a dependency. The package manager uses a package's metadata to automatically install the dependencies. Package managers keep track of what files belong to what packages, what packages are installed, and what versions of those packages are installed.

Installing Software on CentOS, Fedora, and RedHat Distributions

The **yum** command line utility is a package management program for Linux distributions that use the RPM package manager. CentOS, Fedora, Oracle Linux, RedHat Enterprise Linux, and Scientific Linux are RPM-based distributions on which you can use **yum**.

yum search search-string - Search for search-string.

yum install [-y] package - Install package. Use the **-y** option to automatically answer yes to yum's questions.

yum remove package - Remove/uninstall package.

yum info [package] - Display information about package.

To search for software to install, use **yum search search-string**.

```
$ yum search inkscape
Loaded plugins: refresh-packagekit, security
============== N/S Matched: inkscape ==============
inkscape-docs.i686 : Documentation for Inkscape
inkscape.i686 : Vector-based drawing program using
SVG
inkscape-view.i686 : Viewing program for SVG files

  Name and summary matches only, use "search all" for
everything.
$
```

To install software, use **yum install package**. Installing software requires superuser privileges. This means you need to use **sudo** or switch to the root account with the **su** command.

```
$ sudo yum install inkscape
[sudo] password for bob:
Loaded plugins: refresh-packagekit, security
```

```
Setting up Install Process
Resolving Dependencies
--> Running transaction check
---> Package inkscape.i686 0:0.47-6.el6 will be
installed
--> Processing Dependency: python for package:
...
Dependencies Resolved
===========================================================
 Package      Arch   Version            Repository
Size
===========================================================
Installing:
 inkscape     i686   0.47-6.el6         base         8.6 M
Installing for dependencies:
 ImageMagick i686   6.5.4.7-7.el6_5   updates       1.7 M
...
Transaction Summary
===========================================================
Install      21 Package(s)

Total download size: 21 M
Installed size: 97 M
Is this ok [y/N]: y
Downloading Packages:
(1/21): ImageMagick-6.5.4.7-7.el6_5.i686.rpm
...
Installed:
  inkscape.i686 0:0.47-6.el6

Dependency Installed:
  ImageMagick.i686 0:6.5.4.7-7.el6_5
...
Complete!
```

To uninstall a package, use yum remove. Removing software requires superuser privileges.

```
$ sudo yum remove inkscape
Loaded plugins: refresh-packagekit, security
Setting up Remove Process
```

```
Resolving Dependencies
--> Running transaction check
---> Package inkscape.i686 0:0.47-6.el6 will be
erased
--> Finished Dependency Resolution

Dependencies Resolved

==========================================================
 Package    Arch    Version        Repository       Size
==========================================================
Removing:
 inkscape   i686    0.47-6.el6     @base            37 M

Transaction Summary
==========================================================
Remove         1 Package(s)

Installed size: 37 M
Is this ok [y/N]: y
Downloading Packages:
Running rpm_check_debug
Running Transaction Test
Transaction Test Succeeded
Running Transaction
  Erasing    : inkscape-0.47-6.el6.i686      1/1
  Verifying  : inkscape-0.47-6.el6.i686      1/1

Removed:
  inkscape.i686 0:0.47-6.el6

Complete!
$
```

The rpm Command

In addition to the **yum** command, you can use the **rpm** command to interact with the package manager.

rpm -qa - List all the installed packages.

rpm -qf /path/to/file - List the package that contains file.

rpm -ivh package.rpm - Install a package from the file named package.rpm.

rpm -ql package - List all files that belong to package.

```
$ rpm -qa | sort | head
acl-2.2.49-6.el6.i686
acpid-1.0.10-2.1.el6.i686
aic94xx-firmware-30-2.el6.noarch
alsa-lib-1.0.22-3.el6.i686
alsa-plugins-pulseaudio-1.0.21-3.el6.i686
alsa-utils-1.0.22-5.el6.i686
anaconda-13.21.215-1.el6.centos.i686
anaconda-yum-plugins-1.0-5.1.el6.noarch
apache-tomcat-apis-0.1-1.el6.noarch
apr-1.3.9-5.el6_2.i686
$ rpm -qf /usr/bin/which
which-2.19-6.el6.i686
$ sudo rpm -ivh SpiderOak-5.0.3-1.i386.rpm
[sudo] password for bob:
Preparing...          ####################### [100%]
   1:SpiderOak         ####################### [100%]
$
```

Installing Software on Debian and Ubuntu

The Debian and Ubuntu distributions use a package manager called APT, the Advanced Packaging Tool. APT is comprised of a few small utilities with the two most commonly used ones being apt-cache and apt-get.

apt-cache search search-string - Search for search-string.

apt-get install [-y] package - Install package. Use the **-y** option to automatically answer yes to apt-get's questions.

apt-get remove package - Remove/uninstall package, leaving behind configuration files.

apt-get purge package - Remove/uninstall package, deleting configuration files.

apt-cache show package - Display information about package.

To search for software to install, use **apt-cache search search-string**.

```
$ apt-cache search inkscape
create-resources - shared resources for use by
creative applications
inkscape - vector-based drawing program
python-scour - SVG scrubber and optimizer
fonts-opendin - Open DIN font
fonts-rufscript - handwriting-based font for Latin
characters
ink-generator - Inkscape extension to automatically
generate files from a template
lyx - document processor
robocut - Control program for Graphtec cutting
plotters
sozi - inkscape extension for creating animated
presentations
ttf-rufscript - handwriting-based font for Latin
characters (transitional dummy package)
$
```

To install software, use **apt-get install package**. Installing software requires superuser privileges. This means you need to use **sudo** or switch to the root account with the **su** command.

```
$ sudo apt-get install inkscape
Reading package lists... Done
Building dependency tree
Reading state information... Done
The following extra packages will be installed:
  aspell aspell-en cmap-adobe-japan1 dbus-x11
. . .
```

```
3 upgraded, 74 newly installed, 0 to remove and 96
not upgraded.
Need to get 62.7 MB of archives.
After this operation, 171 MB of additional disk space
will be used.
Do you want to continue [Y/n]? y
...
Setting up perlmagick (8:6.6.9.7-5ubuntu3.2) ...
Processing triggers for libc-bin ...
ldconfig deferred processing now taking place
$
```

To uninstall a package, use **apt-get remove**. Removing software requires superuser privileges.

```
$ sudo apt-get remove inkscape
Reading package lists... Done
Building dependency tree
Reading state information... Done
The following packages will be REMOVED:
  inkscape
0 upgraded, 0 newly installed, 1 to remove and 96 not
upgraded.
After this operation, 64.9 MB disk space will be
freed.
Do you want to continue [Y/n]? y
(Reading database ... 69841 files and directories
currently installed.)
Removing inkscape ...
Processing triggers for man-db ...
Processing triggers for hicolor-icon-theme ...
$
```

The dpkg Command

In addition to the **apt** utilities, you can use the **dpkg** command to interact with the package manager.

dgpk -1 - List all the installed packages.

148

dpkg -S /path/to/file - List the package that contains the file.

dpkg -i package.deb - Install a package from the file named package.deb.

dpkg -L package - List all files that belong to package.

```
$ dpkg -l | head
Desired=Unknown/Install/Remove/Purge/Hold
| Status=Not/Inst/Conf-files/Unpacked/halF-conf/Half-
inst/trig-aWait/Trig-pend
|/ Err?=(none)/Reinst-required (Status,Err:
uppercase=bad)
||/ Name             Version
Description
+++-=================-=============-=================
ii  accountsservice  0.6.15-2ubuntu9.6      query
and manipulate user account information
ii  acpid            1:2.0.10-1ubuntu3      Advanced
Configuration and Power Interface event daemon
ii  adduser          3.113ubuntu2           add and
remove users and groups
ii  apparmor         2.7.102-0ubuntu3.9     User-
space parser utility for AppArmor
ii  apport           2.0.1-0ubuntu17.5
automatically generate crash reports for debugging
$ dpkg -S /usr/bin/which
debianutils: /usr/bin/which
$ sudo dpkg -i spideroak_5.1.3_i386.deb
[sudo] password for bob:
Selecting previously unselected package spideroak.
(Reading database ... 153942 files and directories
currently installed.)
Unpacking spideroak (from spideroak_5.1.3_i386.deb)
...
Setting up spideroak (1:5.1.3) ...
Processing triggers for man-db ...
Processing triggers for desktop-file-utils ...
Processing triggers for bamfdaemon ...
```

```
Rebuilding /usr/share/applications/bamf.index...
Processing triggers for gnome-menus ...
$
```

Video on Installing Linux Software

If you would like to see exactly what it's like to install software on a Linux system, check out this video that I put together for you: http://www.linuxtrainingacademy.com/installing-software/

Summary

In this chapter, you learned how packages are typically used to install software on Linux systems. You learned how to manipulate packages with a package manager. Two of the most popular package formats are RPM and Debian. For RPM based distributions, you learned how to use the **yum** and **rpm** commands. For Debian based distributions you learned how to use the **apt** and **dpkg** commands to manage packages.

Resources

* Managing Software with Yum
  https://www.centos.org/docs/5/html/yum/

* AptGet Howto
  https://help.ubuntu.com/community/AptGet/Howto

* Ubuntu - Installing Software
  https://help.ubuntu.com/community/InstallingSoftware

* Installing Linux Software Video
  http://www.linuxtrainingacademy.com/installing/

Quiz

1. The Debian and RedHat Enterprise Linux distributions use the same package format.

    a. True

    b. False

2. How would you search for "apache" using **yum**?

    a. yum search apache

    b. yum find apache

    c. yum get apache

    d. yum-cache search apache

3. Which command lists all of the RPM packages installed on a system?

    a. rpm -a

    b. rpm -q

    c. rpm -qa

    d. rpm -ea

4. How would you install the htop package on a Debian based distribution?

    a. apt-get htop

    b. apt-get install htop

    c. apt-cache install htop

d. yum-get htop

5. Which of the following commands will list the contents of the htop Debian package?

a. dpkg -S htop

b. dpkg –i htop

c. dpkg -l htop

d. dpkg –L htop

Quiz Answers

1. B

2. A

3. C

4. D

VIEWING AND EDITING FILES

Here are some simple commands that display the contents of files on the screen.

cat file - Display the entire contents of file.

more file - Browse through a text file. Press **Spacebar** to advance to the next page. Press **Enter** to advance to the next line. Type **q** to quit viewing the file. Commands are based on the **vi** editor, which is covered in the next section.

less file - Like **more** but allows backward movement and pattern searches.

head file - Output the beginning (or top) portion of file.

tail file - Output the ending (or bottom) portion of file.

This is how you might examine a file named file.txt with the commands **cat**, **tail**, and **more**.

```
$ cat file.txt
This is the first line.
This is the second.
Here is some more interesting text.
Knock knock.
Who's there?
More filler text.
The quick brown fox jumps over the lazy dog.
The dog was rather impressed.
Roses are red,
Violets are blue,
All my base are belong to you.
Finally, the 12th and last line.
$ head file.txt
This is the first line.
This is the second.
Here is some more interesting text.
Knock knock.
Who's there?
More filler text.
The quick brown fox jumps over the lazy dog.
The dog was rather impressed.
Roses are red,
Violets are blue,
$ tail file.txt
Here is some more interesting text.
Knock knock.
Who's there?
More filler text.
The quick brown fox jumps over the lazy dog.
The dog was rather impressed.
Roses are red,
Violets are blue,
All my base are belong to you.
Finally, the 12th and last line.
$ more file.txt
Here is some more interesting text.
Knock knock.
Who's there?
...
```

By default, **head** and **tail** only display ten lines. You can override this behavior and tell them to display a specified number of lines. The format is **-n** where **n** is the number of lines you want to display. If you only want to display the first line of a file, use **head -1 file**. Want to display the last three lines? Then run **tail -3 file**.

```
$ head -2 file.txt
This is the first line.
This is the second.
$ tail -1 file.txt
Finally, the 12th and last line.
$
```

Viewing Files In Real Time

Using **cat** can be a fine way to view files that have fairly static content. However, if you are trying to keep up with changes that are being made in real time to a file, **cat** is not the best choice. A good example of files that can change often and rapidly are log files. For example, you may need to start a program and look at that program's log file to see what it is doing. For this case, use the **tail -f file** command.

tail -f file - Follows the file. Displays data as it is being written to the file.

```
$ tail -f /opt/app/var/log.txt
Oct 10 16:41:17 app: [ID 107833 user.info] Processing
request 7680687
Oct 10 16:42:28 app: [ID 107833 user.err] User pat
denied access to admin functions
. . .
```

Editing Files

Nano

If you need to edit a file right now and do not want to spend any time learning obscure editor commands, use **nano**. Nano is a clone of `pico`, so, if for some reason the **nano** command is not available, `pico` probably is. It's not as powerful as some other editors, but it's definitely easier to learn.

When you start **nano**, you will see the file's contents and a list of commands at the bottom of the screen. To run the commands, replace the caret symbol (^) with the `Ctrl` key. For example, to exit **nano** type `Ctrl-x`.

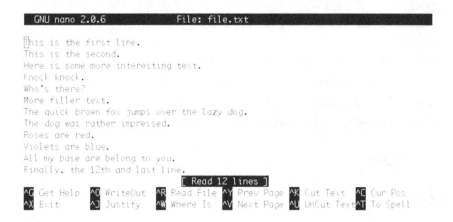

Editing in **nano** is quite easy. The up and down arrow keys will take you to the previous or next lines as expected. The right and left arrow keys let you navigate forwards and backwards on the same line. Simply type the desired text into the editor. To save the file, type `Ctrl-o`. If you forget to save the file before you exit, **nano** will ask you if you want to save the file. To learn more, type `Ctrl-g` for help.

Vi

While **nano** is great for simple edits, **vi** and **emacs** have more advanced and powerful features. There is a learning curve to using these editors as they are not exactly intuitive. It will require a bit of a time investment to become proficient. Let's start by looking at **vi**.

`vi [file]` - Edit file.

`vim [file]` - Same as `vi`, but with more features.

`view [file]` - Starts `vim` in read-only mode. Use `view` when you want to examine a file but not make any changes.

`Vim` stands for "Vi IMproved." It is compatible with the commands found in `vi`. Some of the additional features of `vim` include syntax highlighting, the ability to edit files over the network, multi-level undo/redo, and screen splitting. On many Linux distributions, when you invoke `vi`, you are actually running `vim`.

One advantage of knowing `vi` is that `vi` or a `vi` variant, like `vim`, is always available on the system. Another advantage is that once you learn the key mappings for `vi`, you can apply them to other commands—like `man`, `more`, `less`, `view`—and even your shell.

Vi Modes

Command Mode

`Vi` has the concept of modes. You are always working in one of three modes: command mode, insert mode, or line mode. When `vi` starts, you are placed in command mode. To get back to command mode at any time, hit the escape key (`Esc`). Letters typed while in command mode are not sent to the file, but are rather interpreted as commands. Command mode allows you to navigate about the file, perform searches, delete text, copy text, and paste text.

Here are some commonly used key bindings for navigation.

`k` - Up one line.

`j` - Down one line.

`h` - Left one character.

l - Right one character.

w - Right one word.

b - Left one word.

^ - Go to the beginning of the line.

$ - Go to the end of the line.

Note that commands are case sensitive. For example, if you want to move down one line, type the lowercase **j**. The uppercase **J** joins lines together. The original **vi** editor did not employ the use of arrow keys; however, **vim** does, so you may find that you can use arrow keys on your system. The advantages of learning the original key bindings are 1) they always work and 2) it's faster since your hand does not have to leave the home row.

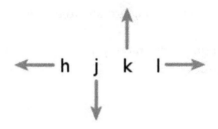

Insert mode

To enter insert mode, press one of the following keys.

i - Insert at the cursor position.

I - Insert at the beginning of the line.

a - Append after the cursor position.

A - Append at the end of the line.

After entering insert mode, type the desired text. When you are finished, type **Esc** to return to command mode.

Line mode

To enter line mode, you must start from command mode and then type a colon (:) character. If you are in insert mode, type **Esc** to get back to command mode and then type a colon for line mode. Here are some of the most common line mode commands you will want to know.

:w - Writes (saves) the file.

:w! - Forces the file to be saved even if the write permission is not set. This only works on files you own.

:q - Quit. This will only works if there have not been any modifications to the file.

:q! - Quit without saving changes made to the file.

:wq! - Write and quit. After modifying a file, this command ensures it gets saved and closes **vi**.

:x - Same as :wq.

:n - Positions the cursor at line **n**. For example, :5 will place the cursor on the fifth line in the file.

:$ - Positions the cursor on the last line of the file.

:set nu - Turn on line numbering.

:set nonu - Turn off line numbering.

:help [subcommand] - Get help. If you want more information on the **:w** command type **:help :w**.

Mode	Key	Description
Command	Esc	Used to navigate, search, and copy/paste text.
Insert	i I a A	Also called text mode. Allows text to be inserted in the file.
Line	:	Also called command-line mode. Save the file, quit vi, replace text, and perform some navigation.

Here is a screenshot of **vim**. Tildes (~) represent lines beyond the end of the file.

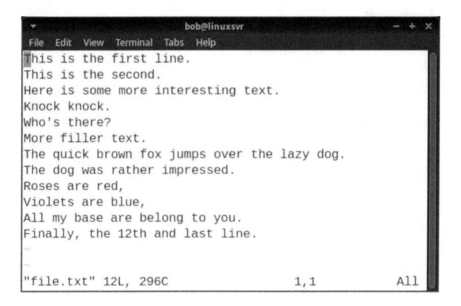

Advanced Editing with vi

You can repeat commands in **vi** by preceding them with a number. For instance, if you would like to move the cursor up 5 lines, type **5k**. If you would like to insert a piece of text 80 times, type **80i** and start entering the text. Once you hit **Esc** to return to command mode, the text you typed will be repeated 80 times. If you would like to make a line of asterisks, you could type **80i*Esc**. Can you start to see how **vi** is more powerful than an editor like **nano**?

Deleting Text

x - Delete a character.

dw - Delete a word. To delete five words, type **d5w**. The repeating concept in **vi** shows up in many places.

dd - Delete a line. To delete three lines, type **3dd**.

D - Delete from the current position to the end of the line.

Changing Text

r - Replace the current character.

cw - Change the current word.

cc - Change the current line.

c$ - Change the text from the current position to the end of the line.

C - Same as **c$**.

~ - Reverses the case of a character.

Copying and Pasting

yy - Yank (copy) the current line.

y<position> - Yank the <position>. For example, to yank a word, type **yw**. To yank three words type **y3w**.

p - Paste the most recent deleted or yanked text.

Undo / Redo

u - Undo.

Ctrl-r - Redo.

Searching

/<pattern> - Start a forward search for <pattern>.

?<pattern> - Start a reverse search for <pattern>.

Tutorial

Run vimtutor from the command line start the vim tutorial.

Emacs

Emacs is another powerful editor. Some people really find themselves drawn to **vi** while others thoroughly enjoy using **emacs**. It's a bit of a rivalry in the Linux world, actually. Experiment with **emacs** and **vi** to see which one works for you. You can't make a bad choice as they are both great editors.

emacs [file] - Edit file.

When reading **emacs** documentation, know that **C-<char>** means to hold down the **Ctrl** key while pressing **<char>**. For example, **C-h** means to hold down the **Ctrl** key while pressing the **h** key. If you see **C-h t**, that means to hold down **Ctrl** key while pressing the **h** key, release the **Ctrl** key and then type the letter **t**.

When you see **M-<char>**, that means hold down the "meta" key, which is the **Alt** key, while pressing **<char>**. You can also substitute the **Esc** key for the **Alt** key. **M-f** translates to holding down the **Alt** key and pressing **f** or pressing and releasing **Esc** followed by typing the **f** key. You may need to use **Esc** for the meta key since **Alt** may be intercepted by your terminal program, for instance. If you want to simplify things, always use **Esc** for the meta key as it will work in all situations.

Here are some helpful **emacs** commands.

C-h - Help.

C-x C-c - Exit. While holding down **Ctrl**, press **x**, continue to hold down **Ctrl**, and press **c**.

C-x C-s - Save the file.

C-h t - Emacs has a nice built-in tutorial.

C-h k <key> - Describe key. Use this to get help on a specific key command or key combination.

Navigating

C-p - Previous line.

C-n - Next line.

C-b - Backward one character.

C-f - Forward one character.

M-f - Forward one word.

M-b - Backward one word.

C-a - Go to the beginning of the line.

C-e - Go to the end of the line.

M-< - Go to the beginning of the file.

M-> - Go to the end of the file.

Deleting Text

C-d - Delete a character.

M-d - Delete a word.

Copying and Pasting

C-k - Kill (cut) the rest of the current line of text. To kill the entire line, position the cursor at the beginning of the line.

C-y - Yank (or paste) from the previously killed text.

C-x u - Undo. Keep repeating for multi-level undo.

Searching

C-s - Start a forward search. Type the text you are looking for. Press **C-s** again to move to the next occurrence. Press **Enter** when you are done searching.

C-r - Start a reverse search.

Repeating

Like **vi**, **emacs** provides a way to repeat a command.

C-u N <command> - Repeat <command> N times.

For instance, to kill three lines of text, type **Ctrl-U 3 Ctrl-k**.

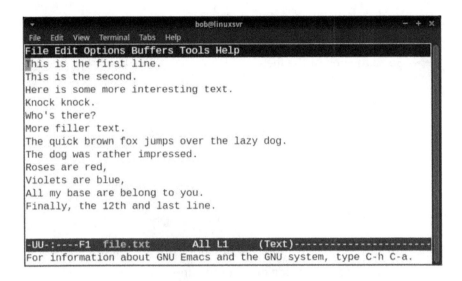

You have only scratched the surface with the **vi** and **emacs** editors. There is so much more to learn if you are interested. Both editors have features that include macros, global replace, and more. Entire books have been written on each of these editors.

Graphical Editors

So far, you have learned about command line editors that are appropriate to use when you connect to a server via ssh. However, if you are running Linux as a desktop operating system you might be interesting in some graphical text editors and word processors. Here are some for your consideration.

- **emacs** - Emacs has a graphical mode, too.

- **gedit** - The default text editor for the Gnome desktop environment.

- **gvim** - The graphical version of vim.

- **kedit** - The default text editor for the KDE desktop environment.

If you are looking for a Microsoft Word replacement, consider AbiWord or LibreOffice. LibreOffice not only includes a word processor, but it is a complete office suite with a spreadsheet program, a database, and presentation software.

If you are looking for a source code editor to aid in computer programming, look at Geany, jEdit, or Kate. Sublime Text is another option. It is a commercial product that runs on Windows, Mac, and Linux.

Specifying a Default Editor

Some commands rely on the **$EDITOR** environment variable to tell them which program to use for editing. Since cron's primary purpose is to schedule jobs, it delegates the task of editing files to another program. The **crontab -e** command invokes the editor specified by the **$EDITOR** environment variable. You can set **$EDITOR** in your personal initialization files to ensure your favorite editor is used, be it **nano**, **emacs**, **vi**, or something else.

```
$ echo $EDITOR
vi
```

Summary

In this chapter, you learned how to view and edit files. First you learned how to display the contents of a file using the **cat**, **more**, **less**, **head**, and **tail** commands. Next you learned how to use the **nano** text editor. From there you were introduced to the **vim** editor. Next, the **emacs** text editor was covered. Finally, graphical text editors were explained.

Quiz

1. Which of the following commands display the first line of the file named "file.txt"?

    a. top file.txt

    b. top +1 file.txt

    c. head file.txt

    d. head -1 file.txt

2. What command would you use to view the changes as they occur to the /var/log/messages file?

    a. watch /var/log/messages

    b. tail /var/log/messages

    c. tail -f /var/log/messages

    d. tail -1 /var/log/messages

3. Use the nano editor if you need powerful and complex editing capabilities.

    a. True

    b. False

4. Which is not a valid vi mode?

    a. command

    b. insert

    c. line

    d. fundamental

5. Emacs can be used as a graphical editor as well as from the command line.

    a. True

    b. False

Quiz Answers

1. D

2. C

3. B

4. D

5. A

Shell Scripting

A script is a command line program that contains a series of commands. The commands contained in the script are executed by an interpreter. In the case of shell scripts, the shell acts as the interpreter and executes the commands listed in the script one after the other.

Anything you can execute at the command line, you can put into a shell script. Shell scripts are great at automating tasks. If you find yourself running a series of commands to accomplish a given task, and know you will need to perform that task again in the future, you can—and probably should—create a shell script for that task.

Let's look at a simple shell script. The name of this script is **script1.sh**.

```
#!/bin/bash
echo "Scripting is fun!"
```

Before you try to execute the script, make sure that it is executable.

```
$ chmod 755 script1.sh
```

Here is what happens when you execute the script.

```
$ ./script1.sh
```

```
Scripting is fun!
$
```

The Shebang

You'll notice that the first line of the script starts with **#!** followed by the path to the bash shell program, **/bin/bash**. The number sign is very similar to the sharp sign used in music notation. Also, some people refer to the exclamation mark as a "bang." So, **#!** can be spoken as "sharp bang." The term Shebang is an inexact contraction of "sharp bang."

When a script's first line starts with a shebang, what follows is used as the interpreter for the commands listed in the script. Here are three examples of shell scripts, each using a different shell program as the interpreter.

```
#!/bin/csh
echo "This script uses csh as the interpreter."
```

```
#!/bin/ksh
echo "This script uses ksh as the interpreter."
```

```
#!/bin/zsh
echo "This script uses zsh as the interpreter."
```

When you execute a script that contains a shebang, what actually happens is that the interpreter is executed and the path used to call the script is passed as an argument to the interpreter. You can prove this by examining the process table.

Let's start this script, **sleepy.sh**, in the background and look at the process table.

The contents of sleepy.sh:

```
#!/bin/bash
sleep 90
```

Let's execute it in the background and take a look at the processes.

```
$ ./sleepy.sh &
[1] 16796
$ ps -fp 16796
UID          PID  PPID  C STIME TTY          TIME CMD
jason       16796 16725  0 22:50 pts/0    00:00:00
/bin/bash ./sleepy.sh
$
```

You can see that what is actually running is **/bin/bash ./sleepy.sh**. Let's use a full path to the script.

```
$ /tmp/sleepy.sh &
[1] 16804
$ ps -fp 16804
UID          PID  PPID  C STIME TTY          TIME CMD
jason       16804 16725  0 22:51 pts/0    00:00:00
/bin/bash /tmp/sleepy.sh
$
```

Sure enough, **/bin/bash /tmp/sleepy.sh** is being executed. Also, you can see that **/bin/bash** is executing the sleep command, which is the first and only command command in the shell script.

```
$ ps -ef| grep 16804 | grep -v grep
jason       16804 16725  0 22:51 pts/0    00:00:00
/bin/bash /tmp/sleepy.sh
jason       16805 16804  0 22:51 pts/0    00:00:00
sleep 90
$ pstree -p 16804
sleepy.sh(16804)——sleep(16805)
$
```

If you do not supply a shebang and specify an interpreter on the first line of the script, the commands in the script will be executed using your current shell. Even though this can work just fine under many

173

circumstances, it's best to be explicit and specify the exact interpreter to be used with the script. For example, there are features and syntax that work just fine with the bash shell that will not work with the csh shell.

Also, you don't have to use a shell as the interpreter for your scripts. Here is an example of a Python script named **hi.py**.

```
#!/usr/bin/python
print "This is a Python script."
```

Let's make it executable and run it.

```
$ chmod 755 hi.py
$ ./hi.py
This is a Python script.
$
```

For more information on python programming and scripting, see my book *Python Programming for Beginners* at http://www.linuxtrainingacademy.com/python-book.

Let's get back to shell scripting.

Variables

You can use variables in your shell scripts. Variables are simply storage locations that have a name. You can think of variables as name-value pairs. To assign a value to a variable, use the syntax **VARIABLE_NAME="Value"**. Do not use spaces before or after the equals sign. Also, variables are case sensitive, and, by convention, variable names are in all uppercase.

```
#!/bin/bash
MY_SHELL="bash"
```

To use a variable, preceed the variable name with a dollar sign.

```
#!/bin/bash
MY_SHELL="bash"
```

```
echo "I like the $MY_SHELL shell."
```

You can also enclose the variable name in curly braces and preceed the opening brace with a dollar sign. Syntax: **${VARIABLE_NAME}**.

```
#!/bin/bash
MY_SHELL="bash"
echo "I like the ${MY_SHELL} shell."
```

Here is the output of the script:

```
I like the bash shell.
```

The curly brace syntax is optional unless you need to immediately precede or follow the variable with additional data.

```
#!/bin/bash
MY_SHELL="bash"
echo "I am ${MY_SHELL}ing on my keyboard."
```

Output:

```
I am bashing on my keyboard.
```

If you do not encapsulate the variable name in curly braces, the shell will treat the additional text as part of the variable name. Since a variable with that name does not exist, nothing is put in it's place.

```
#!/bin/bash
MY_SHELL="bash"
echo "I am $MY_SHELLing on my keyboard."
```

Output:

```
I am  on my keyboard.
```

You can also assign the output of a command to a variable. To do this, enclose the command in parentheses and precede it with a dollar sign.

```
#!/bin/bash
SERVER_NAME=$(hostname)
echo "You are running this script on ${SERVER_NAME}."
```

The output of the command **hostname** is stored in the variable **SERVER_NAME**. In this sample output, the server name is **linuxsvr**.

```
You are running this script on linuxsvr.
```

You can also enclose the command in back ticks. This is an older syntax that is being replaced by the **$()** syntax. However, you may see this in older scripts.

```
#!/bin/bash
SERVER_NAME=`hostname`
echo "You are running this script on ${SERVER_NAME}."
```

Valid variable names

Variable names can contain letters, digits, and underscores. They can start with letters or underscores, but cannot start with a digit. Here are examples of valid variable names.

```
FIRST3LETTERS="ABC"
FIRST_THREE_LETTERS="ABC"
firstThreeLetters="ABC"
```

Here are some examples of invalid variable names.

```
3LETTERS="ABC"
first-three-letters="ABC"
first@Three@Letters="ABC"
```

Tests

Scripts are designed to replace the need for a person to physically sit at a keyboard and type in a series of commands. What if you have a task you want to automate, but it requires different actions based on different circumstances? Since a person may not be around to make decisions when the script needs to run, we'll need to test for those conditions and have the script act accordingly.

To create a test, place a conditional expression between brackets. The syntax is: **[condition-to-test-for]**. You can test for several types of situations. For example, you can compare if strings are equal, if a number is greater than another one, or if a file exists. This test checks to see if **/etc/passwd** exists. If it does, it returns true. In other words, the command exits with a status of 0. If the file doesn't exist, it returns false. I.e., the command exits with a status of 1.

```
[ -e /etc/passwd ]
```

If you are using the bash shell, you can run the command **help test** to see the various types of tests you can perform. You can also read the man page for tests: **man test**. Here are of some of the more common tests you can perform.

```
File operators:
  -d FILE        True if file is a directory.
  -e FILE        True if file exists.
  -f FILE        True if file exists and is a regular
file.
  -r FILE        True if file is readable by you.
  -s FILE        True if file exists and is not
empty.
  -w FILE        True if the file is writable by you.
  -x FILE        True if the file is executable by
you.

String operators:
  -z STRING      True if string is empty.
  -n STRING      True if string is not empty.
     STRING      True if string is not empty.
  STRING1 = STRING2
                 True if the strings are equal.
  STRING1 != STRING2
                 True if the strings are not equal.
Arithmetic operators:
  arg1 -eq arg2  True if arg1 is equal to arg2.
  arg1 -ne arg2  True if arg1 is not equal to arg2.
  arg1 -lt arg2  True if arg1 is less than arg2.
  arg1 -le arg2  True if arg1 is less than or equal
to  arg2.
  arg1 -gt arg2  True if arg1 is greater than arg2.
```

```
    arg1 -ge arg2   True if arg1 is greater than or
equal to arg2.
```

The if Statement

Now that you know how to determine if a certain condition is true or not, you can combine that with the **if** statement to make decisions in your scripts.

The **if** statement starts with the word **if** and is then followed by a test. The following line contains the word **then**. Next is a series of commands that will be executed if the tested condition is true. Finally, the **if** statement ends with **fi**, which is **if** spelled backwards. Here is the syntax.

```
if [ condition-true ]
then
    command 1
    command 2
    . . .
fi
```

Here is an example:

```
#!/bin/bash
MY_SHELL="bash"

if [ "$MY_SHELL" = "bash" ]
then
    echo "You seem to like the bash shell."
fi
```

It is a best practice to enclose variables in quotes to prevent unexpected side effects when performing conditional tests. Here is the output of running the script:

```
You seem to like the bash shell.
```

You can also perform an action if the condition is not true by using an **if/else** statement. Here is what an **if/else** statement looks like.

```
if [ condition-true ]
then
    command 1
    command 2
    ...
else  #
    command 3
    command 4
    ...
fi
```

Let's update the script to perform an action if the statement is not true.

```
#!/bin/bash
MY_SHELL="csh"

if [ "$MY_SHELL" = "bash" ]
then
    echo "You seem to like the bash shell."
else
    echo "You don't seem to like the bash shell."
fi
```

Here is the output. Because **["$MY_SHELL" = "bash"]** evaluated as false, the statements following **else** were executed.

```
You don't seem to like the bash shell.
```

You can also test for multiple conditions using **elif**. The word **elif** is a contraction for "else if." Like **if**, follow **elif** with a condition to test for. On the following line, use the word **then**. Finally, provide a series of commands to execute if the condition evaluates as true.

```
if [ condition-true ]
then
    command 1
    command 2
    ...
elif [ condition-true ]
then
    command 3
    command 4
```

179

```
    . . .
else  #
    command 5
    command 6
    . . .
fi
```

Here is an updated script using **elif**:

```
#!/bin/bash
MY_SHELL="csh"

if [ "$MY_SHELL" = "bash" ]
then
    echo "You seem to like the bash shell."
elif [ "$MY_SHELL" = "csh" ]
then
    echo "You seem to like the csh shell."
else
    echo "You don't seem to like the bash or csh
shells."
fi
```

Output:

```
You seem to like the csh shell.
```

The for Loop

If you want to perform an action on a list of items, use a **for** loop. The first line of a **for** loop starts with the word **for** followed by a variable name, followed by the word **in** and then a list of items. The next line contains the word **do**. Place the statements you want to execute on the following lines; then end the **for** loop with the word **done** on a single line.

```
for VARIABLE_NAME in ITEM_1 ITEM_2 ITEM_N
do
    command 1
    command 2
    . . .
```

```
done
```

Essentially, what happens is that the first item in the list is assigned to the variable and the code block is executed. The next item in the list is then assigned to the variable and the commands are executed. This happens for each item in the list.

Here is a simple script that shows how a **for** loop works:

```
#!/bin/bash
for COLOR in red green blue
do
   echo "COLOR: $COLOR"
done
```

Output:

```
COLOR: red
COLOR: green
COLOR: blue
```

It's common practice for the list of items to be stored in a variable as in this example.

```
#!/bin/bash
COLORS="red green blue"

for COLOR in $COLORS
do
   echo "COLOR: $COLOR"
done
```

Output:

```
COLOR: red
COLOR: green
COLOR: blue
```

This shell script, **rename-pics.sh**, renames all of the files that end in **jpg** by prepending today's date to the original file name.

```
#!/bin/bash
PICTURES=$(ls *jpg)
DATE=$(date +%F)

for PICTURE in $PICTURES
do
   echo "Renaming ${PICTURE} to ${DATE}-${PICTURE}"
   mv ${PICTURE} ${DATE}-${PICTURE}
done
```

Here's what happens when you run this script:

```
$ ls
bear.jpg  man.jpg  pig.jpg  rename-pics.sh
$ ./rename-pics.sh
Renaming bear.jpg to 2015-03-06-bear.jpg
Renaming man.jpg to 2015-03-06-man.jpg
Renaming pig.jpg to 2015-03-06-pig.jpg
$ ls
2015-03-06-bear.jpg  2015-03-06-man.jpg  2015-03-06-
pig.jpg  rename-pics.sh
$
```

Positional Parameters

Positional parameters are variables that contain the contents of the command line. These variables are $0 through $9. The script itself is stored in $0, the first parameter in $1, the second in $2, and so on. Take this command line as an example:

```
$ script.sh parameter1 parameter2 parameter3
```

The contents of $0 is "script.sh", $1 is "parameter1", $2 is "parameter2", and $3 is "parameter3".

This script, **archive_user.sh**, accepts a parameter which is a username:

```
#!/bin/bash

echo "Executing script: $0"
echo "Archiving user: $1"
```

```
# Lock the account
passwd -l $1

# Create an archive of the home directory.
tar cf /archives/${1}.tar.gz /home/${1}
```

Comments

Anything that follows the pound sign is a comment. The only exception to this is the shebang on the first line. Everywhere else in the script, when a pound sign is encountered it marks the beginning of a comment. Comments are dutifully ignored by the interpreter as they are for the benefit of us humans.

Anything that follows the pound sign is ignored. If a pound sign starts at the beginning of a line the entire line is ignored. If a pound sign is encountered in the middle of a line, the information to the right of the pound sign is ignored.

Here is what the output looks like when we execute the **archive_user.sh** script:

```
$ ./archive_user.sh elvis
Executing script: ./archive_user.sh
Archiving user: elvis
passwd: password expiry information changed.
tar: Removing leading `/' from member names
$
```

Instead of referring to $1 throughout the script, let's assign its value to a more meaningful variable name.

```
#!/bin/bash

USER=$1    # The first parameter is the user.

echo "Executing script: $0"
echo "Archiving user: $USER"
```

```
# Lock the account
passwd -l $USER

# Create an archive of the home directory.
tar cf /archives/${USER}.tar.gz /home/${USER}
```

The output remains the same.

```
$ ./archive_user.sh elvis
Executing script: ./archive_user.sh
Archiving user: elvis
passwd: password expiry information changed.
tar: Removing leading `/' from member names
$
```

You can access all the positional parameters starting at $1 to the very last one on the command line by using the special variable **$@**. Here is how to update the **archive_user.sh** script to accept one or more parameters.

```
#!/bin/bash

echo "Executing script: $0"

for USER in $@
do
   echo "Archiving user: $USER"

   # Lock the account
   passwd -l $USER

   # Create an archive of the home directory.
   tar cf /archives/${USER}.tar.gz /home/${USER}
done
```

Let's pass multiple users into the script.

```
$ ./archive_user.sh chet joe
Executing script: ./archive_user.sh
Archiving user: chet
passwd: password expiry information changed.
tar: Removing leading `/' from member names
```

```
Archiving user: joe
passwd: password expiry information changed.
tar: Removing leading `/' from member names
$
```

Getting User Input

If you want to accept standard input, use the **read** command. Remember that standard input typically comes from a person typing at the keyboard, but it can also come from other sources, like the output of a command in a command pipeline. The format for the **read** command is **read -p "PROMPT" VARIABLE_NAME**. This version of the archive_user.sh script asks for the user account.

```
#!/bin/bash

read -p "Enter a user name: " USER

echo "Archiving user: $USER"

# Lock the account
passwd -l $USER

# Create an archive of the home directory.
tar cf /archives/${USER}.tar.gz /home/${USER}
```

Let's run this script and archive the **mitch** account.

```
$ ./archive_user.sh
Enter a user name: mitch
Archiving user: mitch
passwd: password expiry information changed.
tar: Removing leading `/' from member names
$
```

Summary

The first line in a shell script should start with a shebang followed by the path to the interpreter that should be used to execute the script.

To assign a value to a variable, start with the variable name, followed by an equals sign, followed by the value. Do not use a space before or after the equals sign.

You can access the value stored in a variable by using **$VARIABLE_NAME** or **${VARIABLE_NAME}**. The latter form is required if you want to precede or follow the variable with additional data.

To assign the output of a command to a variable, enclose the command in parentheses and precede it with a dollar sign. **VARIABLE_NAME=$(command)**

Perform tests by placing an expression in brackets. Tests are typically combined with **if** statements.

Use **if**, **if/else**, or **if/elif/else** statements to make decisions in your scripts.

To perform an action or series of actions on multiple items, use a **for** loop.

To access items on the command line, use positions parameters. The name of the program is represented by **$0**, the first parameter is represented by **$1**, and so on. To access all the items on the command line starting at the first parameter (**$1**), use the special variable **$@**.

You can place comments in your scripts by using the pound sign.

Accept user input by using the **read** command.

Quiz

1. The first line of a shell script typically starts with a shebang followed by the path to an interpreter that will be used to execute the commands in the script.

    a. True

    b. False

2. Which of the following variables is valid?

    a. 3LETTERS="ABC"

    b. first-three-letters="ABC"

    c. first@Three@Letters="ABC"

    d. FIRST3LETTERS="ABC"

3. What is the value of "$1" given the following command line:

    ```
    $ ./add-user.sh tom richard harry
    ```

    a. ./add-user.sh

    b. tom

    c. richard

    d. harry

4. Which is the proper way to assign a value to a variable?

    a. VAR="VALUE"

    b. VAR = "VALUE"

ASON CANNON

5. Which of the following will assign the output of the **hostname** command to the variable **HOSTNAME**?

    a. HOSTNAME=$(hostname)

    b. HOSTNAME=`hostname`

    c. All of the above.

Quiz Answers

1. A

2. D

3. B

4. A

5. C

Conclusion

Congratulations on making it to the end of the book! We've covered a lot of material along the way. First, you learned about the Linux boot process. Next, you learned about the various types of messages generated by a Linux system, where they're stored, and how to control them.

You also learned how to manage disks and create file systems. We talked about creating and managing users and groups on a Linux system. You learned about TCP/IP networking and how to configure network interfaces on a Linux server. You also learned some techniques to troubleshoot common network problems.

From there you learned how to manage jobs and processes. Next, you tackled the complex subject of Linux file and directory permissions. You also learned how to install and manage software. You were even introduced to shell scripting and learned how to automate tasks on a Linux system.

Again, I want to congratulate you on seeing this book through to the end. I hope you've gained some valuable insights into the world of

Linux administration. I love hearing from my readers. Let me know how this book has helped you and if there is anything I can do for you!

All the best,

Jason
http://www.LinuxTrainingAcademy.com/contact

About the Author

Jason Cannon started his career as a Unix and Linux System Engineer in 1999. Since that time, he has utilized his Linux skills at companies such as Xerox, UPS, Hewlett-Packard, FireEye, and Amazon.com. Additionally, he has acted as a technical consultant and independent contractor for small to medium businesses.

Jason has professional experience with CentOS, RedHat Enterprise Linux, SUSE Linux Enterprise Server, and Ubuntu. He has used several Linux distributions on personal projects including Debian, Slackware, CrunchBang, and others. In addition to Linux, Jason has experience supporting proprietary Unix operating systems including AIX, HP-UX, and Solaris.

He enjoys teaching others how to use and exploit the power of the Linux operating system and offers online video training courses at http://www.LinuxTrainingAcademy.com.

Jason is also the author of *Linux for Beginners*, *Python Programming for Beginners*, and *Command Line Kung Fu*

Other Books by the Author

Command Line Kung Fu: Bash Scripting Tricks, Linux Shell Programming Tips, and Bash One-liners
http://www.linuxtrainingacademy.com/command-line-kung-fu-book

High Availability for the LAMP Stack: Eliminate Single Points of Failure and Increase Uptime for Your Linux, Apache, MySQL, and PHP Based Web Applications
http://www.linuxtrainingacademy.com/ha-lamp-book

Linux for Beginners: An Introduction to the Linux Operating System and Command Line
http://www.linuxtrainingacademy.com/linux

Python Programming for Beginners
http://www.linuxtrainingacademy.com/python-programming-for-beginners

Additional Resources

For even more resources, visit:
http://www.linuxtrainingacademy.com/resources

Books

Command Line Kung Fu
http://www.linuxtrainingacademy.com/command-line-kung-fu-book

Do you think you have to lock yourself in a basement reading cryptic man pages for months on end in order to have ninja like command line skills? In reality, if you had someone share their most powerful command line tips, tricks, and patterns, you'd save yourself a lot of time and frustration. This book does just that.

High Availability for the LAMP Stack
http://www.linuxtrainingacademy.com/ha-lamp-book

Eliminate Single Points of Failure and Increase Uptime for Your Linux, Apache, MySQL, and PHP Based Web Applications

Linux for Beginners
http://www.linuxtrainingacademy.com/linux

This book is the perfect introduction to the Linux operating system and command line. In it, you'll learn the most important fundamentals of Linux.

Python Programming for Beginners
http://www.linuxtrainingacademy.com/python-programming-for-beginners

If you are interested in learning how to program, using Python specifically, this book is for you. In it, you will learn how to install Python, which version to choose, how to prepare your computer for a great experience, and all the computer programming basics you'll need to know to start writing fully functional programs.

Courses

High Availability for the LAMP Stack
http://www.linuxtrainingacademy.com/ha-lamp-stack

Learn how to set up a highly available LAMP stack (Linux, Apache, MySQL, PHP). You'll learn about load balancing, clustering databases, creating distributed file systems, and more.

Linux Administration
http://www.linuxtrainingacademy.com/linux-admin

Learn the skills you need to know in order to become a Linux System Administrator or Linux Systems Engineer and level-up your caraeer today!

Learn Linux in 5 Days
http://www.linuxtrainingacademy.com/linux-in-5-days

Take just 45 minutes a day for the next 5 days and I will teach you exactly what you need to know about the Linux operating system. You'll learn the most important concepts and commands, and I'll even guide you step-by-step through several practical and real-world examples.

Python Programming Course
http://www.linuxtrainingacademy.com/python-course

This comprehensive course covers the basics of Python as well as the more advanced.

Shell Scripting
http://www.linuxtrainingacademy.com/shell-course

Learn all of my bash scripting and coding secrets in this course.

APPENDIX: TRADEMARKS

BSD/OS is a trademark of Berkeley Software Design, Inc. in the United States and other countries.

Facebook is a registered trademark of Facebook, Inc.

Google is a registered trademark of Google Inc.

Firefox is a registered trademark of the Mozilla Foundation.

HP and HEWLETT-PACKARD are registered trademarks that belong to Hewlett-Packard Development Company, L.P.

IBM® is a registered trademark of International Business Machines Corp., registered in many jurisdictions worldwide.

Linux® is the registered trademark of Linus Torvalds in the U.S. and other countries.

Mac and OS X are trademarks of Apple Inc., registered in the U.S. and other countries.

Open Source is a registered certification mark of Open Source Initiative.

Sun and Oracle Solaris are trademarks or registered trademarks of Oracle Corporatoin and/or its affiliates in the United States and other countries.

UNIX is a registered trademark of The Open Group.

Windows is a registered trademark of Microsoft Corporation in the United States and other countries.

YouTube is a registered trademark of Google Inc..

All other product names mentioned herein are the trademarks of their respective owners.